better
together

🐾 spotted dog press

Better Together:
Strengthen Your Family, Simplify Your Homeschool,
and Savor the Subjects that Matter Most

PamBarnhill.com

ISBN 978-0-9997421-0-5 (print), 978-0-9997421-1-2 (epub)

∴ spotted dog press

Editor
Ann Karako

Publishing and Design Services:
MartinPublishingServices.com

better together

strengthen your family,
simplify your homeschool,
and savor the subjects
that matter most

PAM BARNHILL

spotted dog press

Contents

Foreword

While reading Pam's book on Morning Time, it occurred to me that I do not have nine children; I have ten. And I don't mean my husband, even though he is quite nervous that with no more children to homeschool I will commence teaching him. No, I feel that my tenth child, the darling I anxiously watch from afar to see how it flourishes, is Morning Time.

To see the idea of Morning Time slowly take root over many long years and finally to reproduce itself in a new generation is astounding to me.

To say that I created Morning Time because we participated in it for so many years is like saying I created breakfast because we had oatmeal every day. Still it is a much-loved adopted child, and to see it thrive in old and new ways is gratifying. I think this is happening now, after so many years, just because it is so organic, so natural. If you are in the business of ordering affections (*ordo amoris*) then Morning Time is the most obvious, if not the easiest, way to go.

Twenty-seven years ago Timothy (my oldest) and I repeated his Awana verse, sang a Bible song, read nursery rhymes, and read aloud all morning long just because it was so much fun. Then we got up the next day and did it again. We never did stop.

This past school year was our last official year of Morning Time. Andrew and Alex and I got up many mornings, prayed together, read poems, diagrammed sentences, then read *The*

Iliad and *The Odyssey* together. It was a fitting way to end a quarter century of family tradition.

Only it is not the end. If Pam is right and we are not merely teachers but fellow travelers, then it makes sense that Morning Time will continue for me. I will still get up and seek the Lord in His Word, sing His praises, and commence praying for my husband, my nine children, their four spouses, and my ten grandchildren. Many days I will read a poem, and most days I will read a few chapters from a few books. Turns out Morning Time might have just been an excuse for me to learn after all. Nothing has changed except that no toddler interrupts me these days, except when the grandchildren are visiting. This week two little girls have kept me from my devotions but not from participating in a liturgy of love. As I sat reading aloud to them from the book my grandmother read aloud to me, I couldn't help but get choked up. Love is a liturgy. It means something. I must tell someone.

People used to ask me to write a book about Morning Time. For awhile I thought maybe I would, but then I didn't, and life got complicated. Then one day I looked up and I was not the only one. The burden was lifted. Other women— writers, mothers, teachers—were writing and living out their own Morning Times. Sarah MacKenzie breathed new life into my posts, and now Pam has written this helpful book. And helpful it is. It even made me a little sad that I couldn't do it all over again. However, Pam's reminder that I am still a learner encouraged me.

Pam has said so much that I would say and then some. I love reading about Morning Time from her fresh perspective. So much of her experience is common to my family. Once upon a time I had three little children and we had Morning Time just like Pam! Then there were nine, and then eight, and then seven, and so on just like an Agatha Christie mystery. And now suddenly, so suddenly, just two are left at home but going on to other schools of life. Yet Morning Time lives on in my life, in Pam's family, and maybe in your family too. That brings me great joy. "I have no greater joy than to hear my children walk in the truth" (I John 1:4).

Thanks, Pam, for reminding me of the fun I had with my children once upon a time. May the fruit last long after you and I are gone.

Cindy Rollins,
Summer 2015
Preface to the first edition

part
one

one

A Homeschool Wish List

When I first became interested in the concept of homeschooling my kids, I rarely doubted that I could actually *do* it. I mean, I had taught for years in inner-city high schools and middle schools. I won awards, gave workshops for other teachers, and had former students who later told me that my classes were the ones that had most prepared them for the real world. While I wasn't the flashiest teacher—in fact, looking back, I can think of over a million ways I could have been a much better one—I was competent and confident in my ability to do my job. Homeschooling would be no different, I thought.

Then I actually started homeschooling. While teaching a class of high school freshmen how to write compelling news stories is no easy feat, I found that homeschooling is an entirely different emotional experience. As a public school teacher, I had been committed to my students. Being solely responsible for the education of your own child, though, is the kind of thing that keeps you up at night—many nights.

That is not to say that doing the job of homeschooling—and it *is* a job—is not worth the sleeplessness. The rewards of getting to spend your days as a family, experiencing the moments when wonder and learning collide, and allowing your kids time to play and be kids, far outweigh the hours spent working and worrying.

I have always had an affinity for hearing other people's homeschooling stories. I love the "day-in-the-lifestyle" vignettes on blogs that give a glimpse into what others' homeschool days look like. A few years ago I turned this interest into a podcast called *The Homeschool Snapshots Podcast*. Each 30-minute episode consists of about 20 minutes when I ask the homeschooler who is being the guest that day the very same questions on each show. Who is your favorite homeschool guru? What would you tell your younger self? How do you go about salvaging a bad homeschool day? I don't do this because I can't think of anything else to ask, but instead I do it for reassurance.

The message I want parents to get from listening to the show is that there is no single right way to homeschool. Different families will thrive under different circumstances or will follow different educational philosophies. Yet we are so much more alike than we are different. We have similar hopes and dreams for our kids and are striving for similar goals—educating healthy, happy, productive adults who are well-adjusted to live in this fallen world. We also have similar struggles—like those annoying, all-too-frequent, bad homeschool days.

Today is Not the Definition of Your Homeschool

Kortney Garrison spent two-and-a-half years serving indigenous people in Suriname. Now armed with a library card and her own intense curiosity, she homeschools her three young kids in the Pacific Northwest. She reminded me in a recent *Snapshots* interview that one day is not the sum total of your homeschool experience, even though it can very much seem like it when you are in the muddle. "Whether (today) is a really amazing day or a less amazing day, one day doesn't make or break you. We are here for the long haul, and this is a big journey that we are on," Kortney said.[1]

As hard as that is to remember on the good days, it is much harder to remember on the bad ones. On the bad ones we are certain we are ruining our children's lives (and possibly that they are ruining ours as well). Homeschool Frustration Syndrome is a very real thing, despite the fact that I just made up that name. You wake in the morning uneager to even begin your day. You face whining kids who drag their feet and don't want to start. You worry that your homeschooling is ineffective. The kids are not retaining any of the information that is in their textbooks. You despair that your homeschool is boring and joyless. They aren't interested in the material you are presenting at all. You don't blame them—you don't much like it yourself.

When you first began researching homeschooling, you encountered the blogs of moms who incorporated nature journaling, learning about great art, and listening to beautiful music in their homeschools. Within their families they sang hymns, memorized scripture, and read beautiful poetry together. You wanted all of those things for your homeschool; but reading lessons, math worksheets, history texts, dirty diapers, and toddler messes soon turned into "How does anyone ever have time for all those extras?"

You feel as if your day is an exercise in checking boxes,

with one day as monotonous as the next. You want education to be more than selecting the best pieces to pad a portfolio. Your interactions with your kids have been reduced to fights over finishing the math worksheet; and speaking of fights, your kids' interactions with each other consist largely of those. Where is the relationship? Where is time to build character, to teach articles of your faith? You wonder how to get it all done each day. School is time-consuming! Everyone is going about their own tasks. There has got to be a way to teach multiple ages at once, but it eludes you. The school day drags on into the late afternoon, or tasks don't get finished at all.

Whoa, mama. Take a deep breath.

What's Your Homeschool Makeover Wish List?

My entire family loves to watch the TV show *Fixer Upper*. From Dad down to the seven-year-old boy, there is something about the show that appeals to each of us. On the show the husband-and-wife team of Chip and Joanna Gaines show a family three rundown houses. The family selects one of the three, and then the Gaines spend the rest of the show turning that house into something stunning. My kids mostly love the antics of crazy Chip Gaines. I think my husband is drawn in by the craftsmanship and carpentry (he has a desk job, and secretly, I think, he would rather work with his hands). As for me, the appeal of the show is the promise of the "after." The Gaines take something that is tired, dated, and clearly not working, and turn it into something that the homeowners find beautiful, functional, and perfect for their needs.

That's the beauty of a makeover. What was once

disorganized becomes functional. What was once tired becomes energized. What was once drab becomes beautiful. There is a point in each show when the guest family declares what is on their wish list for their new home. They itemize their needs. It is up to the show's makeover team to be sure that the new home has those features. What about you? If you could make a homeschool wish list, what might it include? How would you go about fighting Homeschool Frustration Syndrome in your home?

For our family, the cure has been about establishing a time in our day when we can all learn together. A time where the oldest (me!) down to the youngest can study largely from the same curriculum, be read to from the same books, and contemplate the same ideas—each to their own ability. It has been about creating a space for shared discussion and presenting truths that are education for the old just as much as for the young. It has been about using simple but powerful methods as old as education itself—methods like listening to stories, questioning and discussing, telling back, and recitation. It has been about adding beauty and delight to our day to feed our souls and keep us going. All of the above are on my homeschool wish list, and fortunately I have a found a practice that allows me to easily add them to our day.

It is called Morning Time.

Two

Rage Against the Daily Grind

Being hugely pregnant with twins had seriously disrupted Angela Boord's sleep schedule. She had settled on being happy if she woke by eight, because then she knew that she would at least get her school day going by nine. She savored those few minutes to herself before her 8-, 6-, and 2-year-olds were ready to get up. That time meant that she would be able to take a shower without the toddler telling her indignantly that she was standing in his tractor field when she stepped onto the bath mat.

By 9:00 am everybody was *usually* eating breakfast. Angela knew this probably sounded like a hideously late hour to many people, but the twin pregnancy had her in survival mode. Grabbing a bite and a small stack of books, she began reading to the kids while they ate. This helped them to wake up, and it gave her some time to recover from the efforts of taking a shower, making breakfast, and getting the two-year-old *to* the breakfast table. They read from *Egermeir's Story Bible* until everyone was done eating, then they switched to the couch and read another selection—usually history or literature. Sometimes the kids drew or modeled clay; sometimes they didn't.

The practice—which Angela dubbed "Morning Time" somewhere along the way after reading about similarly-named practices from homeschool bloggers like Cindy Rollins, Jennifer Mackintosh, and Kendra Fletcher—has become the backbone of Angela's homeschool.

"It just sort of grew up from what we needed. The twins were born, and you're just busy *all* the time; but then right after the twins, my next child is only 22 months younger. He's like the third twin. When you're dealing with so many little people, you're thinking, 'OK, if the day goes totally wrong, what should I have done?' I want to feel some sort of accomplishment with the day. We will say our prayers; we're going to read from the Bible; we're going to do a catechism question. If we get that done, then it all feels better, because we have done *something*. If there's still more time, because things aren't totally self-destructing at that point, we'll add some read-alouds, maybe some history. If we got 45 minutes, it was good. We didn't do any math or anything like that, but we got a good chunk of something done in our day."[2]

Twelve years later there is a new house in a new state, five more kids, and the 8-year-old has since graduated and moved on to college; but the reading aloud is still the beginning of Angela's homeschool. There have been periods during the intervening years that she eliminated the practice due to the stress of wrangling toddlers, health issues, moves, and family illness; but it has always returned as a staple of their day.

"It's like a touch point; it's an anchor in everybody's day. When it's gone, everybody's sort of adrift. It can't be gone for too long, or the kids will start asking about it. 'When are we going to start again?'—and even the teenagers, they'll just go automatically and sit down on the couch and wait. It becomes like an institution in your life."[3]

Like Angela and many other homeschoolers, I also started this extraordinary daily practice in an unextraordinary way. Looking back, I can't quite remember how I stumbled onto the idea. There are posts from a few years ago on my own blog that make vague references to beginning but tell no story of origin. Most likely I read about it on Cindy Rollins's now-defunct *Ordo Amoris* blog or the blogs of other homeschoolers, and I was inspired by their enthusiasm to give it a try myself. What I came to realize after a few years of implementing my Morning Time, though, was the power of this simple practice—even if it doesn't take place in the morning.

As I spoke to blog readers and podcast listeners, it soon became apparent that there were many moms out there who were looking for a way to enjoy homeschooling more as well as feel like they were actually succeeding at teaching their kids. Let's face it—homeschooling can be a little bit of a grind. Math and phonics must be practiced daily. Kids whine and complain. Mom worries. And for every brief, shining moment of wonder or academic exhilaration (love those!), there are many, many stressful moments of juggling kids, subjects, and skills that need to be learned.

Like Angela discovered, what we need is some kind of homeschool super-practice. Something that does the double duty of helping us teach our kids all the things we never learned during our own educations and want very much to share with them—while at the same time allowing us to use our time wisely and tick off science, history, or even critical thinking and grammar, for multiple ages. And oh yes, it should be so joyful that everyone can't wait to start, finishes with a good attitude, and feels likes their voice has been acknowledged and heard. Morning Time can do all that. Really.

While Morning Time had its origin in classical and Charlotte Mason homeschooling circles, it has gained recent widespread popularity in the homeschooling community with its inclusion as a key strategy in Sarah Mackenzie's book *Teaching from Rest*. Once I began writing and podcasting about Morning Time, moms told me over and over that they had been doing similar practices for many years, without giving it a name. It is no surprise that an idea so good—one that highlights relationship and efficiency—would spring up independently in homeschools around the world. I believe the practice is the best thing any mom—classical, Charlotte Mason, unit study, school-at-home, or even unschooler—can bring into her home.

Homeschool Well and Still Enjoy It

As homeschool moms, our days are long, and our burden is not often light. We worry about how to get homeschooling done and do it well. After all, we want our children to be good people—successful and productive members of society. As teachers and mothers, we have taken the responsibility for their education on ourselves, and it weighs heavy. Add to that the fact that we have to spend hours every day working on subjects we were happy to put aside after our own school years, and homeschooling can quickly and easily become mundane and rote. Morning Time helps us combat all of these feelings. The efficiency of Morning Time allows us to introduce the entire family to many more ideas than we could ever experience working independently. The enjoyment we derive from the content gives us something to look forward to in our day-to-day. Morning Time eases our homeschooling burden by providing us a place for excellence and enjoyment.

Many people focus on the fact that Morning Time allows them to fit in the extra subjects that they enjoy but never find time for elsewhere. This is so true, but Morning Time is also an efficient way to arrange the subjects you *need* to do. If you are doing a literature-based curriculum (*Sonlight* or *My Father's World* are two examples), then Morning Time is the place to put many of your read-alouds. It's the spot for history and nature study (science for little kids). It's not just a location for the "extras" but a place to get the required things done.

We need practices that save us time and energy. While for some subjects students must be divided by ability level—most of our students will always have their own math book, handwriting, or spelling—many subjects can be done together as a family. There is really no such thing as third grade history or science. Instead, use Morning Time as a way to teach these subjects to many multi-age children at one time. The key to whole-family learning is to find engaging material to read together, do group narrations and discussion, and add extra expectations for older children, such as additional independent reading or written narrations.

In addition to science and history, there are a number of other subjects that are easily done in a group during Morning Time. What about geography? Map work can be done together at each student's ability level. Include some living books about the region and a handicraft if your students are so inclined, and you have an easy geography study. The same is true for religious instruction (read from the Bible or catechism for even the youngest students) or even English grammar. Younger students can identify nouns, verbs, and adjectives, while older students diagram the same sentence on the whiteboard. Never underestimate the value of younger students "tagging along" as you discuss concepts with older kids. They will soon surprise you with how much they remember and understand.

It's About Ideas

Learning should be a time for contemplation and discussion—unhurried, free from anxiety, and full of wonder. So often our schoolwork has a tendency to be reduced to the utilitarian. We complete curriculum and check off lists, learning necessary skills with little thought to life-giving learning practices. The ritual and pace of Morning Time forces us to slow down, enjoy, and savor ideas as we encounter them together.

Learning does not have to be about lists of questions, blanks to complete, or bubbles to fill. Instead, it can be just children, a masterful storyteller, and a bit of contemplation. One of my children's favorite activities for Morning Time is to play with homemade play dough as they listen to Jim Weiss read *Story of the World*. Occasionally, one of them makes a profound comment about the story, and I am struck that they have been listening with great care. We might even turn the recording off at this point and have a brief discussion.

There are times weeks later that they hear something which reminds them of one of these stories, and they point it out to me. They have obviously been thinking about the reading, and they make a connection to these ideas which have been planted in their minds and their imaginations. This is learning at a much higher level than simply completing a workbook page.

So much of our school days are centered around facts. Sure, it is good to know that London is the capital of England, that the area of a rectangle is equal to its length times its width, and that the Declaration of Independence was signed in 1776. Yet knowing the date of the Declaration's signing does not teach children about freedom, unalienable rights, or the duty of a people to throw off an oppressive government. Those are ideas, and they make us think. Sonya Shafer of *Simply Charlotte Mason,* a resource site for homeschoolers who follow the Charlotte Mason method of education, tells us that ideas are "common human experiences and emotions that we can relate to and learn from."[4] Whereas facts are dry and easily forgotten, ideas are grasped, shared, and remembered.

Morning Time, by its design, is a perfect forum for exposure to a wide feast of ideas. Through the books they read, the music they hear, and the words they hide in their hearts, students come in contact with great thinkers; they become part of the Great Conversation. Charlotte Mason tells us in *Towards a Philosophy of Education,*

"Education is a life. That life is sustained on ideas. Ideas are of spiritual origin, and God has made us so that we get them chiefly as we convey them to one another, whether by word of mouth, written page, Scripture word, musical symphony; but we must sustain a child's inner life with ideas as we sustain his body with food."[5]

And while that may seem a rather lofty goal for a 21st-century homeschool mom, it really doesn't have to be. Author Sarah Mackenzie shared with me in a recent podcast interview how she does this. "So in my very ordinary home with my very ordinary kids—and I'm a very ordinary homeschool mom, not very impressive as far as what I do with my kids on a day-to-day basis—how do I make these big ideals fit into our ordinary life? Morning Time is how I do it."[6]

Irrigating Deserts

Great thoughts are not easily digested. They take a bit of work to comprehend, work that we as humans sometimes resist. This is why Augustine says we must teach our children to "love what is lovely."[7] This means exposing them to things that we know are good, true, and beautiful on a consistent basis. Through careful listening and regular exposure, we train their ear to love beautiful music and faithful hymns. Through discussion and observation, we help them see the harmonious use of line, color, and texture in art. Through the reading of scripture, fairy tale, and myth, we shape their moral imagination. In the *Abolition of Man*, C.S. Lewis laments modern education's focus on the cultivation of the mind at the expense of cultivation of affections:

"For every one pupil who needs to be guarded from a weak excess of sensibility, there are three who need to be awakened from the slumber of cold vulgarity. The task of the modern educator is not to cut down jungles, but to irrigate deserts."[8]

In our culture, children are exposed to characters like Bratz dolls and Spongebob; for many children that may be the only "art" they ever view. As parents we must counteract the entertainment culture with what is truly lovely. Our job is not just to shape their intellect, but also to flood their affections with beauty. Morning Time is a space carved into our day to introduce the beautiful ideas found in music, art, and great thoughts.

A Community of Learners

So many of us, myself included, were formed with a public school mindset. This philosophy, which permeates our culture, says that kids of a certain age should learn with kids of the same age, and the lines should not be blurred. As homeschoolers, the problem we face is that typically, barring multiples or adoption, we have only one child of any given age in our home at any given time. This means that our tendency is for our children to do much of their learning in isolation—one student reading one work of literature, learning one writing skill, mastering one math concept. Each child is very busy building his or her own storehouse of knowledge.

Morning Time allows us to gather our community of learners together to share the same stories, poems, and ideas. We can read and discuss together. Old and young alike have the opportunity to sip at the chalice of knowledge. Ideas must be wrestled with, and there is no better way to do this than in community. Discuss, disagree, find evidence to support your brother's argument, form your own theory. Should Fern have saved the runt pig? What would happen in our society if books were banned completely? Should Napoleon have invaded Russia? By carefully thinking about our responses to questions and defending them, we will come to own the truths embodied in each idea.

Embrace the Flexibility

Morning Time activities also can serve specific purposes for homeschoolers who follow various homeschooling methods. Unit study homeschoolers will find that Morning Time is a perfect fit into what they do already. The heart of both unit studies and Morning Time is learning in community, after all. This is where unit study homeschoolers will be able to do the bulk of the reading for their current study.

School-at-home homeschoolers will find that Morning Time is a good place to bring the family together for a few subjects. Also, school-at-home curricula have a tendency to skimp on those beautiful, humanities-based subjects like art and music. Do those in Morning Time, instead.

Relaxed homeschoolers or unschoolers can appreciate Morning Time as a place to ensure minimum instruction for the day. Read *Life of Fred* or some other living math book, play a math game, do a few *Mad Libs* or some freewriting, read a bit from a history or nature book and then turn the kids loose to pursue their interests for the day. This bit of enjoyable, "stealth" family learning can ease mom's mind when she worries, "Am I doing enough?"

The flexibility of Morning Time is perhaps one of its greatest assets. It can mean different things to different families and serve different purposes—sometimes even within a single family. The Morning Time you have when your oldest is six, and you have a passel of preschoolers, will not resemble your Morning Time five or ten years later—nor should it.

In an ideal world, an atmosphere of contemplation and discussion of beauty and ideas would be our normal mode of interaction with our children. I don't know about you, but my world is far from ideal. Between the laundry, the math worksheets, and my own introverted, type-A personality, these things need a designated time and space in order to flourish in our homeschool. If your personality and circumstances allow you to practice these things organically throughout the day, then go for it and be thankful. If you are more like me and need to name this practice in order to own it, then grab your planner and come with me.

Three

Just One Hour

Sopping paintbrushes filled with water hit the deck with a resounding slap punctuated by contented squeals. Three toddlers—twin boys age two, and a curly-headed older sister, age three—happily "paint" the sunny deck under the watchful eye of their mom. Homeschool mom and speaker Sarah Mackenzie is a fireball of energy, but she often resorts to tactics like porch painting and popsicles in high chairs to be able to squeeze in Morning Time each day. Nearby her three older children bounce on the trampoline or pace the deck rail as if it were a balance beam as they sing their history timeline. Sarah knows she is on the clock. Before long the little guys will tire of painting, and outnumbered and outnoised, the rest of the family will have to stop Morning Time for the day—ready or not. Despite her unpredictable stopping point, she persists in pursuing Morning Time each day.

"Morning Time itself has become a more important part of our school day the more kids we have, especially when we had all three babies in about a year and a half. Ever since then, one of the most important parts of Morning Time for me has just been [that it is] a way to organize ourselves so that we still get to those really wonderful, beautiful, delightful things that we want to do all together in a reliable fashion. Morning Time just makes it happen every day, or most days at least."⁹ Sarah's Morning Time didn't always look this way.

"We would actually, at one point when it was just the three older kids, start our day with Morning Time, before we had breakfast. Everybody would kind of stumble out to the living room in our pajamas, and we'd all get coffee or hot chocolate or whatever, and sit down. Then I'd start with our read-aloud. For the next two hours (breakfast would kind of get woven into it), we would read aloud from a very wide variety of books. So we'd read 20 minutes from our liturgy book, and we'd also do some memory work; we'd also do some Shakespeare, we'd also do some geography, and we would do a lot more because we had a lot more time. I do miss that. I loved doing that. I know that is not my season right now. We're making Morning Time work in a way that fits with our family season, but it still has the same function of being the placeholder for those things that are so important that I don't want them to slip through the cracks—a place to put first things first."¹⁰

Morning Time does allow us to focus on those things that would otherwise get pushed aside. Where do I schedule a subject like composer study? Picture study? An hour of reading aloud? These are things that we desire to do in our homeschools because we know they are the best of the true, good, and beautiful, or because they are lacking in our own education; but they often get pushed off the schedule for math or grammar or spelling. And what about that math? In our efforts to stay on track and complete each level at its designated pace, do we ever teach our children about the beauty of Fibonacci numbers or the golden mean? What about exploring symmetry or patterns in numbers? Who has time for that, you say? That's the beauty of Morning Time. It is the time when we can pull out and admire all these glittering gems that might otherwise be lost.

But What Does It Look Like?

While Morning Time will look different in every family, there are some characteristics that are common across most Morning Times. I call them the 3 Rs: Ritual, Reading, and Recitation.

Ritual

One of the primary characteristics of Morning Time is the inclusion of ritual. Ritual elevates mundane, ordinary activities into something that has meaning beyond the sum total of those activities. Why does this matter? After all, aren't we just teaching history and science? No, we are teaching persons. We are striving to help our children become life-long seekers of knowledge by building habits and virtues. Small daily rituals are how we do this.

The consistent, daily habit of Morning Time itself is a ritual. Simply by getting up and doing it day in and day out, you are emphasizing the importance of learning. Some families will begin each Morning Time with prayer, singing, or the reading of Scripture. Each morning session could also begin by lighting a candle or reciting a favorite family poem.

I begin and end our Morning Time each day with the

words of Christ, "Peace be with you." To which my children respond, "And with your spirit." We are reminded of the peace of Christ and that we are to share it with each other throughout the day. This simple practice adds meaning—through ritual—to our morning.

Reading

The heart of Morning Time is what you choose to read aloud to your children. The selection will differ from family to family but will characteristically include the best stories from children's and classic literature, as well as works you all simply enjoy. While each family member may have their own personal reading at other times of day, reading during Morning Time is done in community, which leads to the opportunity for shared discussion.

If you have a wide age range, read books aimed towards the older children first, while everyone is fresh and attention is high. Little ones can play with toys (hopefully; this does take some training, depending on their ages) while you read. Later the older children can be dismissed to complete independent work, and you can take the little ones aside to enjoy stories that will appeal more to them.

The beauty of this family reading program is that with practice, the entire family—from oldest to youngest—will grow in appreciation of beautiful stories and language. It never ceases to amaze my husband that all three of my children yell, "Ooo, Shakespeare!" whenever the author's name is mentioned, as if they are greeting a long-lost friend.

Recitation

Another subject included in many Morning Times is recitation or memorization. Because our character is shaped by the words we hide within our heart, recitation is a valuable method of education in the homeschool. As with every other Morning Time practice, families will approach memory work differently. Scripture, poetry, prayers (in English and Latin), and Shakespeare are all worthy additions to a Morning Time recitation list.

Some families will choose to memorize more, while others may limit themselves to Scripture or poetry. Some families will add practical tidbits such as a history timeline and math facts to this list. For ideas about what to memorize, the list in the appendix will get you started.

The Fourth R

If the 3 Rs are the methods we use to build our Morning Time, the goal behind these practices is the fourth R—relationship. Morning Time is about the ideas and discussion we share, coming together as a family with Mom modeling lifelong learning for her children, building a common family culture that continues to connect us long after our homeschool days are over. Morning Time is for the long view—equipping our children with ideas they will have available to them far into the future. The habits we build, the materials we recite together, and the stories and ideas we encounter shape us, both together and apart.

four

Don't Start Your Day with Math

I've heard the advice, and I'm sure you have, too: you should always start your day with math. They say kids need to tackle difficult subjects while their brains are fresh. They say kids need to get the hardest thing out of the way first. They say kids need to eat that frog so they don't procrastinate. Poppycosh.

I am all about personal productivity and doing hard things first to get them out of the way, but let me let you in on a little secret: *homeschooling has very little to do with personal productivity.* Homeschooling is about relationships. Instead of beginning your days with a struggle that may involve butting heads and damaged relationships with one or more of your children (ask me how I know), you can fill their tanks, and your own, by beginning the day with delight.

When you start your day with something that delights you and your children, they are more eager to begin the school day, and so are you. That is where Morning Time comes in.

It has been said that in order for a child to learn from a teacher, he must first know that the teacher cares about him. There is a deep, emotional need for kids to have a connection with their teacher—even when that teacher is Mom, and we could safely assume the connection is already there. I make a special point to hug each of my children each morning. Yet, despite the morning hugs my kids and I share, we can quickly become separately busy, running off to do chores and working on individual school checklists.

As a homeschool mom with many kids at many different levels, it is inevitable that at some point I will begin to outsource student learning to independent reading, DVDs, and online courses with the brief daily check-in. It is important that children learn to work on their own, but this transition often happens at a time when children need those human relationships more than ever—the adolescent years. The wonderful thing about Morning Time is that it ensures that our education is never fully void of relational learning. It sets apart a time during the day when teacher and student— mother and child and siblings—are learning in community, sharing a common curriculum with the opportunity to discuss the most important ideas.

Jen Mackintosh has been doing Morning Time in her home for about thirteen years. She has seen the impact that Morning Time has had on the relationships in her family, with older kids becoming role models for younger ones.

"What I didn't expect was that the investment that I made with my oldest children would yield this tremendous fruit in terms of habit development with my younger kids— and that worked itself out in our Morning Time most of all. You'd have an older child paired with a younger child, and I'd be reading aloud. That younger child would be a bit antsy or maybe want to ask a question or maybe get up to do something disruptive, and the older child could come alongside and say, 'Oh we're going to do lessons just a few more minutes, so just sit right here.' I really didn't have to teach the younger ones [about Morning Time behavior]; of course you have to reinforce good habits and virtue building, but the example that the older children brought to the table in terms of habit was pretty extraordinary."[11]

Angela Boord has seen similar benefits in her children's relationships due to Morning Time. In her home, it becomes an opportunity for older kids to form answers to tough questions and be able to verbalize them.

"When you have conversation with people ranging from 18 down to the five-year-old, they (the little ones) will ask why, or what about this, or I don't understand; and the teenagers have to really think. I think that's good for everybody, because it helps people to really know what they think about various things; and we do have some meaty conversations dealing with theology or politics or history. That's something they would miss out on if I said, 'OK, you can just go ahead and do your assigned work over there while we're over here doing the other stuff.'"[12]

Mom as Fellow Learner

In this learning community, Mom is both a facilitator of and a participant in Morning Time. In order to foster the kind of relationships I want with my kids, I can't use this time to check my email, send texts, or fold laundry. I have an obligation to my children to be fully present and participating as a co-learner with them. Some days it is so hard. By removing distractions—turning off notifications, shutting all apps except those that are necessary for playing music, etc.—then I am able to focus on the task at hand.

This is important because what I want to do during Morning Time is model being a student to my students. This is not material that I am teaching *to* them—the 3 Rs of Morning Time are not about a transfer of knowledge from teacher to student. Instead, this is material that I am learning *with* them. I benefit just as much from the Scripture, the poetry memorization, and the beautiful music as they do. I benefit from it far more than I ever will benefit from slogging through long division for the fourth time in my life.

Jen knows the impact her participation in Morning Time has on her kids.

"I think that the Morning Time has shown me that I can have the eyes of a child when reading any of our books, reading poetry, learning Shakespeare. I'm a child all over again, modeling that kind of wonder—and it's sincere, it's not forced. The kids get that. It makes it so that it's less of a lesson and more of a relationship."[13]

A mom's role as fellow learner should also dictate the tone of the Morning Time discussion. In her talk, "The Long Haul: On Morning Time," Cindy Rollins cautions heavily against moms using Morning Time discussion as a time to moralize or force agendas. She discourages moms against over-spiritualizing and advises them to "get out of the way" and let the Bible or other readings speak for themselves. Her contention is that if left alone with good material—truth, goodness, and beauty—children can and will wrestle with it and come up with their own right conclusions and connections.[14] Charlotte Mason also advises against interference, calling on teachers to practice the "art of standing aside." In *School Education,* she gives an example:

"The child who learns his science from a textbook,

though he go to Nature for illustrations, and he who gets his information from object-lessons, has no chance of forming relations with things as they are, because his kindly obtrusive teacher makes him believe that to know about things is the same thing as knowing them personally; though every child knows that to know about Prince Edward is by no means the same thing as knowing the boy-prince. We study in many ways the art of standing aside."[15]

All of our lectures merely get in the way of the knowing of a subject. With us too much in the way, a child may know *about* a great many things. What we want instead is for the child to know those things within himself. In order to do this we avoid the lecture and sermonizing. Instead we use techniques like narration and discussion—not a rapid-fire litany of questions, but instead open-ended, thought-provoking prompts. Instead of "What words does Charlotte spin in her web about Wilbur?" we ask, "How was Charlotte a good friend?" Then we sit and wait for children to speak first, without jumping in to provide our own answer to the question. I try to remember that my default mode during these times should be listening and not speaking. It helps to keep my bossy tendencies (I am a first-born INTJ, after all) in check.

Practically Speaking

Another aspect of relationship in Morning Time is much more practical. This is the Morning Meeting, where mom takes the time to talk together as a family about the day's schedule, expectations, habit training, and even simple behavioral reminders. As children grow and become more independent in activities, it is important to discuss practical matters such as who needs a ride to an activity or will be taking the car. Even with younger children, though, it is good to spend a few minutes going over the daily schedule so that their expectations of what the day holds line up with your own. It makes for much smoother sailing when they have an idea of how the day will unfold.

The Morning Meeting is also a time for a bit of habit training—reminders to throw away the empty milk container, be kind to your little brother, or put the toilet seat down. The audience is present and captured, so take advantage of the moment for a few short, simple words outside of the heat of the moment. These reminders are proactive instead of reactive. If it's applicable, take the time to remind them of behavioral expectations for a visiting guest or trip later that day. This is also not a time for sermonizing, for there is no quicker way to lose the attention of that captive audience. Instead, this 3-5 minute opening calmly takes care of the business of the day before it is forgotten or must be shouted hastily in the flurry of activity.

A mom wears many hats; but, if she is wise, the one she wears often and wears well is that of a coach. Set out the game plan, motivate the team, get everyone headed toward the same goal line. We are coaching our kids on the path of virtue. Stratford Caldecott writes in *Beauty in the Word*, "Love is the beginning and end of education, because love is the way we become more human."[16] Through Morning Time we learn to be more human together.

five

On Bed-Making and Beauty

Every morning, without fail, I make my bed. It is not something I even consciously consider each day; it is a practice born from decades of habit. When I was a young child, my mother required me to do this task even on days I took more time protesting than actually making the bed. Not only did she require that the bed be made, but she also required that it be made well—without slip-shod work, the covers hanging askew, or the pillows piled haphazardly on top. Now I like having a made bed. It makes me grumpy to walk through my room when my bed isn't made—things look out of place, messy, and undone.

Do I think making my bed makes me a more virtuous person? Well, yes, I actually do. I know there are those who may not agree with me (read: non-bedmakers); but I do think doing something each day ritually, especially something not fun or exciting, is good for me. Honestly, I wish my ritual morning habit was exercise, because then I could be both virtuous *and* skinny; but any cultivation of discipline makes us better persons. Over 2000 years ago, Aristotle said that good habits, ritual activities, begat virtue.[17] Aristotle and my mom—you can't go wrong with that kind of instruction.

So how do we use Morning Time to grow in virtue? First, we start by doing Morning Time faithfully. Even with my own well-established habit of Morning Time, there are days that I struggle to get started. Maybe someone is out of sorts, or I know the afternoon is busy so I want to just rush through the school day. Other times we have already begun independent work, and it seems like a Herculean effort just to find a good stopping point for everyone. It could also be Satan. No, I am not going all Church Lady on you; I am saying this in all seriousness.

Morning Time is just that rich. Spending an hour beholding truth, goodness, and beauty is the last thing Satan wants us doing each and every day in our home. I have no doubt that he is there throwing up obstacles at every opportunity. So we must simply start each day. Even if we whisper that we are only going to do five minutes. Even if we only do prayer. Even if we don't begin with prayer at all but go straight to everyone's favorite part, whatever that may be. *Beginning is a huge victory over darkness.* Post that on a sticky note somewhere you can see it and live it daily.

Truth and Goodness and Beauty—Oh My!

Many of the world's greatest minds have wrestled with the ideas of truth, goodness, and beauty and come away unsatisfied with their answers. Who am I, then, to be the one to tell you what they are about? Before we can add these ideas to our Morning Time, however, we must know what they are.

It is my hope that my simple explanation will do two things. First, if you are unfamiliar with truth, goodness, and beauty, I hope that my attempt at defining them will begin your path to understanding. Second, I want to spur you on to further explore these concepts using the resources quoted in this chapter. I have no doubt that any human's quest for wisdom about these three things is lifelong and never-ending.

Truth, goodness, and beauty are known as "transcendentals." These ideas can be traced back to Plato and Aristotle, and they were wrestled with mightily by medievals such as St. Thomas Aquinas. The transcendentals (there are five total) are properties of being—objective realities whose meaning is not dependent on religion, culture, or ideology. Nor are they subject to our feelings, senses, or emotions. They exist apart from humanity completely, because they exist within God Himself. The study of these is what the branch of philosophy known as "ontology" is about. Let's take a look at each one more closely to shed further light on them.

Truth

C.S. Lewis defines truth in *The Abolition of Man* as "… the doctrine of objective value, the belief that certain attitudes are really true and others are really false, to the kind of thing the universe is and the kind of things we are."[18] He calls this truth the Tao, thus giving it a nickname, if you will. He rightly shows that the Tao is not subject to any one culture or religion but recognized as truth by many. In fact, in the appendices of *Abolition*, Lewis lists multiple versions of the same truths from various religions and cultures to demonstrate that they are universal and absolute.

As Christians, however, it is easy for us to see exactly what truth is. In John 14:6, Jesus himself said, "I am the way, the truth, and the life..."[19] and in 2 Samuel 7:28 we are told, "Since you, Lord God, are truly God and Your words are truth."[20] God cannot deceive us—He *is* truth. So when we teach our children about God, we teach them about truth. And when we teach them about universal truths, we are truly teaching them about God.

Goodness

In *Beauty in the Word,* Stratford Caldecott explains that "the good is that which is, at any given moment, appropriate, fitting, and right in relation to the objective situation."[21] That is, the good tells us what the right thing to do in a given situation is. As a Christian people, we are guided by the Ten Commandments and the teachings of Jesus, so we know what our actions should be. Goodness is manifested through virtue, which simply means right acting. Our practice of virtues such as compassion, responsibility, duty, self-discipline, honesty, and friendship all reveal goodness.

My faith tells me that as parents we educate our children in goodness by building habits of virtue, for good acts strengthen the virtue within us. We can read stories of compassion, self-discipline, and friendship during Morning Time; but we should also practice those virtues by learning to pay attention while the story is being read or by taking time to help a brother find a specific page, instead of making fun of his confusion. We must not only learn what the right thing to do is, we must also do it.

Another part of the education of goodness is the formation

of conscience. The *United States Catholic Catechism For Adults* explains that, "Conscience is a judgment of reason by which the human person recognizes the moral quality of a concrete act."[22] Formation of conscience is a lifelong endeavor that is done through study and prayer. The reading of Scripture, moral tales, acts of prayer, and moral discussion will all form the conscience of each student as well as that of mom.

Beauty

In *Beauty for Truth's Sake,* Stratford Caldecott defines beauty as "…the radiance of the true and good, and it is what attracts us to both."[23] Yet beauty is a bit of a sticky wicket, because it is so much more difficult to remove from the realm of the subjective than truth or goodness. For us beauty is so closely related to taste that it becomes difficult to separate the objective from the subjective. Let me offer two litmus tests that may help.

First, Caldecott relates an experiment by artist Christopher Alexander. In the test, Alexander asks people to answer six questions in order to compare two objects chosen at random. The last of these questions asks which of the two things they would be happier to offer to God.[24] To me this is the crux of the discussion about whether beauty can be objective or whether it is merely a matter of taste. There are things which I would not prefer to hang in my home or listen to at length because of a personal preference, but that does not mean I find them unworthy to offer to God. My mother's taste in clothing or jewelry varies greatly from my own. That doesn't mean the things I buy her are any less beautiful simply because I do not prefer to wear them myself.

Second, in his book *Six Great Ideas,* Mortimer Adler poses one definition of beauty as something that is well-made and admirable.[25] Each year Christians from the city of Bethlehem visit our church selling holy statues, nativities, and crucifixes. The money they raise goes to support Christians still living in the Holy Land. Of the things they sell, there are a number that I would love to own and have in my home if money would allow—in fact, I have a beautiful crucifix I purchased one year. On the other hand, there are a few items they offer that do not appeal to me. Despite the fact that I find these items less to my taste, I cannot escape the fact that they are well-made, exhibiting admirable craftsmanship. These items are beautiful, whether or not I desire them personally.

Our education in beauty begins in learning to love what is beautiful. The child may prefer noisy cartoons to quiet galleries of beautiful artwork, but with repeated exposure and shared exploration of color, line, and shape, the child will come to appreciate the artwork over time. My two oldest children (we won't discuss the five-year-old) love to go to the art museum. On any given day they have different tolerance levels for wandering and viewing the artwork, but they do look and appreciate. This is because no one has ever told them it is "uncool" or that as children they should not understand what art means. We take it as a matter of fact that we can simply look at and enjoy the art—maybe pointing out a piece we like in particular or asking a question about something that catches our attention. This has not come about because of any great artistic knowledge I have, but simply because I have presented art as a matter of fact— something to be viewed and enjoyed.

So how then do we reconcile our own journey of learning

what is true, good, and beautiful with our need to present it to our children? After all, if we don't have much experience in consciously finding these things ourselves, how can we then point them out to others? We can start with the certain. Holy Scripture, hymns, stories of the saints, and music and artwork that glorify God are all safe bets for that which exhibits true, good, and beautiful.

The trick, though, comes in stretching to help our children see these traits in things that are not overtly religious in nature. If we do not do so, then we place God in a box labeled "religious only" and fail to convey that He is indeed everywhere and has a hand in everything in our world. Any nugget that you find which is true, any character whom you find with a modicum of good, any object that you consider has a bit of beauty, these all glorify God—whether you find them in poem, novel, Greek myth, fairy tale, picture book, song, chant, or nursery rhyme.

Our role as educator and parent is two-fold. First, we must continue to refine our own understanding of the true, good, and beautiful through widening our own exposure to music, art, and literature. That means we must actively pursue knowledge through study and reading widely; and we must continue to pray, form our own conscience, and practice virtue, not only as an example to our children but for our own understanding. Second, we must present this feast of ideas to our children on a regular basis in order to form their own understanding. Repeated exposure and discussion will help them learn to discern the very best of the world.

part

two

six

The Real Power Hour
— Practicing Ritual

J en Dunlap is used to people who stop and stare at her family. With six adopted children from countries as diverse as Russia, Korea, and St. Vincent in the Caribbean, Jen jokingly says she has her own "United Nations" at home. After bringing all these kids home, the Catholic homeschooling mom began praying a morning rosary with her brood and gradually added reading and memorization to their daily meeting. What the time together lacked, though, was a catchy name.

"I used to say, 'Come on, let's do our stuff!' I wanted a name that would appeal to all of our ages and stages and knew that 'Morning Time' wasn't going to fly with my teen. Sometimes we do it at different times of the day."[26] The name she settled on is perhaps one of my favorite monikers for Morning Time. She calls it her "Power Hour." It seems fitting that something called Power Hour would begin with prayer.

Morning Time, though, can be more than a simple prayer

practice. Morning Time has the power to have a shaping and lasting effect on our entire worldview.

In his book *Desiring the Kingdom*, modern philosopher James K.A. Smith explains that people are created to love. In our deepest being we direct our affections towards something and love it. If you know your catechism, then you know the thing we ought to order our affections towards is God; but Smith contends that so often even when we think our desires are ordered rightly, they actually are not. Cultural liturgies—the mall with its culture of consumption, our favorite football team, even overt patriotism—capture our affections and desires and turn them away from God.

Smith's assertion is that we will love what we do on a regular basis—our habits, our ritual actions, shape us and order our loves.[27] The Catholic Church has known this for over 2000 years. That is why even the smallest parish has daily Mass, and the faithful pray the Liturgy of the Hours—prayers at seven set times throughout the day. These practices point our hearts towards God.

This is also why Morning Time is a liturgy. These small practices done daily over time are not only a means to an education (and a good one at that), but they are a means to shaping virtue in ourselves and in our children.

Here are more ideas for building ritual and right affections into Morning Time:

- Start your Morning Time with some small action to indicate that Morning Time has begun. For our family this is the lighting of a candle. Other families begin by ringing a bell to call everyone to Morning Time or with a ritual greeting like, "The Lord be with you."

- Sing praises to God. Begin with a favorite hymn or praise song. I find music is one of those things that puts me in a right mindset for both worship and learning.

- Spend some time focusing on prayer and Scripture, asking for God's grace upon your homeschool day. Spend time in His Word. Your family's preference might be a morning offering or a family devotion time.

- Take time to remember others. We have a space in Morning Time to speak intentions aloud, praying for family and friends (and often dogs) we know. Some families use the photo Christmas cards they receive, bringing out one a week during the year as a reminder to pray for that family.

- Focus on gratitude by having everyone share aloud one thing for which they are thankful.

- You can use Morning Time to ask for forgiveness.[28] Because we are learning in community, this is a good time to seek pardon from those we might have wronged. If your children are like mine, you will have to train them to understand this period is not for casting accusations, but for waiting quietly to see if anyone's heart is moving them to speak. Often we mothers are the ones who need to begin.

- Bless your children. End your morning time with a small prayer asking God to watch over your children for the day.

- Sing the "Doxology" at the close.

You will not do all of these. Choose a couple that you feel would most benefit your family. If your faith tradition has other practices, then by all means substitute those that are most meaningful to you. Also, do not try to begin by doing a big, long list of rituals. Start with one, let it become habit, and then add more if you wish. By constantly lifting our face towards God every day, He becomes part of our everyday life.

From now on at the end of each chapter, I will share snapshots of other families' Morning Times. These interviews will help give you an idea of how Morning Time can look in a variety of families.

Morning Time Snapshot #1:
Angela Boord

How many kids do you have and what are their ages?

I have eight kids—seven boys and one girl. My oldest is 18 and will be attending college in the fall, but the others are all still at home. My daughter is 16, and the younger boys' ages are 12, 9 and 9 (identical twins), 8, 5, and 2.

How long have you been doing Morning Time?

For at least ten years. I was pregnant with twins, and we were in the process of moving a thousand miles from St. Louis, Missouri, to a small town in upstate New York; and I found myself needing to spend a lot of time on the couch in the mornings. I had three kids at the time—ages 8, 6, and 2—and they would gather their drawing paper and coloring books and crayons and sit on the floor of the living room and draw as I read. They didn't want to stop after our normal Bible reading time, so I began to add read-alouds like Laura Ingalls Wilder's *Little House* series and nature study and science titles like the *One Small Square* books.

From there it was relatively convenient for me to add anything to this time that I really didn't want to miss, as our days got crazier and crazier after the twins were born... and then my sixth child twenty-two months later. Some days Morning Time was most of what we did all day! But we managed to get through a surprising amount of reading in all subjects because we did it consistently (usually with a couple of toddlers crawling all over me as I read).

What do you call your Morning Time?

It doesn't really have a name in our house. It begins when I say, "Time to say prayers!" Because that's the first thing we do when we all gather together for our time in the morning; we pray. Sometimes that's all we do, but the kids know that if we have time, we will not just say prayers; we will also read some books. It's been going on for so long that I guess it doesn't really need a name. But I usually use the phrase "Morning Time" when I talk about our morning family work with other people, because it's a lot less confusing.

Typically how long does your Morning Time take on an average day?

Forty-five minutes seems to be a good time for us. Sometimes we will go on for up to an hour and a half if everybody's interested, but it's hard to sustain everybody's attention and keep the little ones out of trouble for more than forty-five minutes. (Actually, keeping the little ones out of trouble for the whole forty-five minutes is pretty impossible, but usually by that time we've reached everyone's limit.)

There are plenty of times, though, when we start late, or the teenagers have too much work, or we have to be somewhere, or everyone's sick, that our Morning Time only lasts between 15 and 30 minutes. On those days, I usually just focus on faith—saying our prayers, maybe going over the Latin prayer we're memorizing, talking about the saint of the day, and then getting a handle on where everyone's day is headed. I usually have our subjects prioritized in my head, and if our time is short, I just go in the order of importance.

What is your favorite Morning Time subject or activity?

I'm not sure I have one! I like it when the kids get involved and ask for "one more chapter," or when they hear something that sparks a connection with something else they've been thinking about; and then suddenly you're in a discussion involving Shakespeare, Alexander the Great, the Just War Doctrine, and the X-Men, with the eighteen-year-old and the eight-year-old trading opinions.

Those conversations don't happen every day, but I think that the garden-level conversations we do have every day are probably just as important (if not more), because they indicate to me that grappling with ideas—not just swallowing and regurgitating them—has become a habit in our family.

What is your kids' favorite Morning Time subject or activity?

That changes from year to year and from kid to kid. Last year the big hit—which surprised me—was Logic. I used *The Fallacy Detective* by Nathaniel and Hans Bluedorn, which is designed to be done together as a family, and I slated it for Morning Time two days a week when my teenagers didn't have early classes. I expected my oldest three (12th grade,

10th grade, and 6th grade at that time) to pay attention, but I never expected the response my then-3rd-grade twins gave the book!

They would pick it up and read ahead when we were done. We had great discussions, and the learning stuck such that various kids will still call out fallacies they recognize in TV commercials, presidential debates, and dinner time conversation with their siblings.

What is your biggest struggle with Morning Time?

I'm going to cheat and mention two, because they are both about equally big. The first struggle I have is trying to accommodate kids of all ages, from age five or so all the way through high school. When it comes to material, I usually try to shoot for the middle, or to use classic literature with a wide appeal. For instance, I think that this year I am going to read Washington Irving's "Rip Van Winkle" in Morning Time. It's listed on *Ambleside Online's* Year 4, but I see no reason that it wouldn't "count" for my sixteen-year-old's high school literature, and my five- and eight-year-olds will probably pick up something from it, too.

Another problem when there are teenagers in the mix is that they have a lot to do. Often they're enrolled in outside classes—either online or outside of the home—and trying to organize Morning Time around their schedules can be difficult. In my experience, teenagers tend to take work for outside classes a little more seriously than work from Mom, so they can be a little impatient with Morning Time if they have a lot of work to do for those classes. To deal with the problems we were having, we only have Morning Time with everyone on the days when my teenagers don't have morning classes. The other days, I keep Morning Time at the same time and just focus on the younger boys.

The other struggle I have had with Morning Time for years is keeping the little ones quiet and calm enough so that I can read. When my big kids were younger, I had everybody get something to do before they sat down; but even when everybody has something to do, that doesn't guarantee that everyone will be calm and quiet. At this point, I think I've learned to tolerate a certain level of chaos. It used to make me want to give up, but over the years I have seen enough fruit in spite of it to know that it's probably more important just to carry on than it is to have a perfectly attentive audience.

What are some of your favorite Morning Time resources?

I think my favorite Morning Time resources are the booklists shared by other homeschool mothers and various homeschooling sites on the web. In particular, I rely heavily on *Ambleside Online* for ideas.

Aside from the titles I mentioned above, a few of our favorite Morning Time read-alouds over the years have been:

- *Black Ships Before Troy* by Rosemary Sutcliffe
- *Tom Sawyer* and *Huckleberry Finn* by Mark Twain
- *The Blessed Friend of Youth: Saint John Bosco* by Neil Boyton
- *Egermeier's Story Bible*

Another resource I like for Catholic homeschoolers is *Saints for Young Readers for Everyday*, which comes in two volumes, one for January - June, the other for July - December. The biographies are short and geared to an upper elementary reading level, but the books work very well for a variety of ages in Morning Time.

What are some of the ritual practices you include in Morning Time?

Our Morning Time always begins with me calling out, "Time to say prayers!" Then we all gather in the front room to say our prayers. After prayers, we usually check the liturgical calendar to see which saint's feast day it is, and then we go over any memory work—Latin, times tables, etc.

If I am just reading to the younger boys, I read from a story Bible at this point; and then we go on to our read-alouds, which may be literature, history, nature study, or faith-based. Depending on the time we have, everyone's attention span, and the length of the chapters, I will read a chapter, section, or poem from one to three books.

Before everybody leaves the room, I make sure to touch base with them about their plans for the day. We are relaxed classical/Charlotte Mason homeschoolers and mix the pursuit of individual interests with assignments in the areas which my husband and I consider important.

How have you seen Morning Time bear fruit in your home?

Although the kids do learn a lot from the material that we cover in Morning Time, I see most of the "fruit" in the form of family togetherness, especially as children grow into the teen years. Sometimes when you have teens and little ones, it can feel as if you're raising two different families.

The teens have outside classes and social engagements and jobs. At home, they spend a lot of time working on their own. It can feel like you barely see them all day, even if they're still in the same house. Morning Time brings everyone together, if only for half an hour or an hour. In the strictly practical sense, it allows me to get a sense of what everyone has going for the day, since we do usually talk about our plans. But it also, I think, helps to build a sense of who we are as a family.

Everyone hears the same books and says the same prayers during that hour. We all talk to each other—about more than Legos or video games or TV shows or why Child X should not be allowed to unload the dishwasher because he always puts the cups in the cabinet wrong. Morning Time helps to build and solidify our common foundation. The prayers we say and the books we read help to strengthen our sense of who we are as a family.

seven

At the Heart of It All
— Enjoying Reading

Audrey Wilkerson's family grew from three children to eight children in the short span of two years. While finalizing the adoption of their three girls from the Democratic Republic of Congo, the Wilkersons found themselves pregnant with baby number seven, and number eight followed soon after. Faced with three second-language learners—not to mention two children under age two—Audrey turned to Morning Time to quickly acclimate her new family members to the English language.

Each morning the family sang hymns, did memorization, and then had an extended period of reading aloud. This primarily consisted of a rotation of Bible reading, poetry, and Shakespeare. They also read often from their favorite novel selections—the *Little House on the Prairie* series and *Anne of Green Gables*. They read from *A Child's Garden of Verses*; sometimes the girls would go to sleep at night with the poetry playing in their room on an iPad. Later they read *Macbeth* and *A Midsummer's Night Dream* in adapted versions for children, and by that time the girls understood a lot of English and found the latter to be pretty funny. None of this is what one might expect to use to teach non-English speakers the language, but to Audrey's delight it worked in spades.

"It's just amazing how those young brains can pick up a language as difficult as English so quickly and at such a young age. I really attribute it to the stories, the literature, the reading aloud, and hearing the vocabulary. It was all very rich—the poetry and Shakespeare. I think so many times we discount how much our young children are picking up when we're reading above their level; but they're still hearing it, and it's getting into their mind and into their heart. I think it definitely has an impact, and it comes out in their vocabulary, in their play, and their imagination."[29]

Reading aloud is something many of us begin when children are very young. I have photos of me reading board books to my daughter when she was just weeks old, and we have been going strong ever since. For many of us, reading to children is intuitive. Stories are something we enjoy, so it stands to reason that they would enjoy them, too. Others of us have heard that reading aloud is vital to a child's development and are committed to the task for that reason. We read to our children to share ideas with them, to inspire curiosity and wonder, and to shape their moral imagination as well as the culture of our family.

The Living Book

This leads to the question of *what* we read during all of this reading aloud time. And the answer is that we read the very best books—the books that feed a child's curiosity and wonder. Charlotte Mason calls these "living books," as opposed to textbooks or books written by committee. These living books are written by a single author and share not only facts but also ideas with our children. They can be fictional stories or nonfiction passages about history, science, or faith.

Sonya Shafer from *Simply Charlotte Mason* says, "The simplest definition of a living book is a book that makes the subject come alive to you. Usually it is written by one author who has a passion for that subject, and it's usually in story form or in conversational tone; and the big difference is that you will be able to see the action or the descriptions in your mind's eye. It will inspire the imagination that way. And usually it will also touch the emotions so that the child will grab hold of it and make it their own; and then it will be much easier to... 'replay the movie in their mind's eye,' which makes it very easy to narrate."[30]

Morning Time reading will be more like rich cream instead of skim milk—so thick with ideas that it is best taken in small servings. Choose books from which you can read a small section and then allow the children the time to work through these ideas in their minds. In fact, some families choose to save longer stories to enjoy during a separate read-aloud session during the day. There is no right or wrong answer to how much you read during Morning Time and how much you read elsewhere. Do what works best for your family; but do consider choosing a few rich, creamy pieces to read early in the day, while minds are fresh and ready to wrestle with the ideas.

When considering which ideas to present, be aware of the moral imagination. The moral imagination is that part of ourselves that recognizes truth, goodness, and beauty, without us even being aware that this recognition is taking place. In his book *Awakening Wonder*, Stephen Turley calls (moral) imagination, "the location in the human soul where our intellectual, moral, and aesthetic experiences are integrated into a harmonious whole, such that the totality of our experiences can be synthesized and expressed in a Christ-centered intellectual, moral, and spiritual life."[31] We are looking for stories that speak to this part of ourselves, stories that form us and teach us about good and evil, right and wrong, virtue and vice.

Scripture is full of such stories, but do not forget fairy tales and folktales of various cultures, as well as symbolic stories like *The Chronicles of Narnia*. Through stories like "Sleeping Beauty," we learn that death is only temporary, and we can be awakened again by the efforts of a worthy prince. *Narnia* teaches us to both love and fear our Sovereign. Even simple stories like the "Three Little Pigs" convey that hard work is a worthy endeavor. None of these stories are overtly preachy; but through repeated exposure to such tales, we will shape our children's inner view of the world.

On the Importance of Sharing Stories

Shared reading also shapes the family culture. Shared stories—our own and those we read aloud—are what make a family a community. They are the common threads that hold us all together. An Aussie homeschool mom of ten, Erin Hassett determines her favorite family read-alouds not just by the quality of the literature but also by the memories the books conjure. She remembers reading *Caddie Woodlawn* when her oldest was eleven. All the children snuggled around her on the couch and begged for chapter after chapter. In the family's memory, *The Complete Tales of Beatrix Potter* is forever tied with a rainy afternoon after the birth of a new sibling.[32]

Sayings and phrases from books are tied up in my own family culture. We never eat roast beef—always roast beast. We tease our little hobbits about their second breakfast. Any made-up game the children play, especially those with ever-changing and elaborate rules, is referred to as "Calvin ball" (from *Calvin and Hobbes* fame), and we sing "jamma-jamma-jamma-jamma-PJ!" (*Pajama Time* by Boynton) when it is time to get ready for bed. These memories we share connect us in ways that go far beyond our biological ties and into our collective being. They are part of the very nature that makes us family.

When creating a read-aloud practice for Morning Time, there are a number of things to take into consideration:

- Families with younger children will gravitate largely towards picture books, both fiction and nonfiction; but do not forget poetry (don't be intimidated!), fairy tales, and fables.

- Families made up of older children and teens can use Morning Time to tackle upper-level works or those that require discussion and discernment. Keep in mind that with older kids, Mom can be relieved of some of the burden of being the lone reader. In fact, elocution and expressive reading are skills easily practiced when giving everyone a turn to read.

- Mixed-age families will want to read to both ends of the age spectrum. Do not underestimate how much upper elementary children will still enjoy a nostalgic read of picture books, so don't hesitate to include some books for the younger set in your daily reading for everyone. You may also be amazed at how much a younger child can understand of a work that should be above his head, even when it seems like he is not listening but is only playing nearby as you read.

- Do not be afraid to be creative with your reading schedule for Morning Time. You can read to the older set first and then release them to work on independent work while you continue reading to the younger children—or vice versa if that works best in your family. Not all family reading for the entire day needs to be crammed into this space. Any time is a good time to read.

- Like any homeschool curriculum or practice, reading in Morning Time should be your servant and not your master. The amount of reading aloud you do in your Morning Time will be different than it is for other families. It will also be different in different seasons of your family life, and that is okay.

What to Read

Ideas for reading aloud during Morning Time can include:

- Biography

- Classic literature

- Classic and modern children's literature (chapter books)

- Fables

- Fairy tales

- History (both historical fiction and nonfiction)

- Nature and science books

- Picture books

- Plays

- Plutarch

- Poetry

- Religious, saint, and missionary stories

- Scripture and Bible stories

- Shakespeare

Resources for Narration and Discussion

I have a few favorite resources for getting the most out of reading during Morning Time.

For both fiction and nonfiction, a good practice to help

children own what has been read is to use oral narration. There are a couple of different forms of narration. The classical model of narration outlined in Susan Wise Bauer's *The Well-Trained Mind* focuses on summarizing the most important parts of the reading. It is aided by leading questions which help children get to the vital facts presented. This is a precursor to learning to summarize for writing.[33]

An alternate form of narration is Charlotte-Mason-style narration. In this version students are asked to tell back not just a summary but everything they remember about the passage. This allows students to work through and wrestle with the ideas in what was read. Sonya Shafer from *Simply Charlotte Mason* tells us, "Charlotte said each child's narration will be a reflection of their personality. They add little delightful touches in there."[34] Only by doing this can children truly know those ideas and call them their own. An excellent resource for this kind of narration is *Your Questions Answered: Narration* by *Simply Charlotte Mason*. This book walks you step-by-step through how to do narration and even gives tips for doing narration in a group setting.

Another great resource is *Teaching the Classics* from *The Center for Lit*, a website dedicated to helping homeschool moms teach literature. This helpful guide by Adam and Missy Andrews includes a DVD series of lectures that teaches parents to see the elements of literature for themselves and then teach them to their own children. This non-intimidating method starts every age group with picture books to see the elements of a story. The resource also comes with a handy guide that includes extensive book recommendations plus a list of over 100 questions that can be used with any story.

Another approach to asking questions can be found in

Sarah Mackenzie's *QuickStart Guide to Great Conversations with Your Kids About Books*. This short and handy guide provides you with five simple questions you can ask your kids about any book you are reading. The questions are sure to get family discussion (and maybe even debate) flowing as you read. The questions require kids to put on their thinking caps, make comparisons, and support their assertions based on evidence from the books. The seven-page guide is easy to read and implement and comes with a set of bookmarks with the questions printed right on them, so you will always have a good discussion-starter handy as you read.

Morning Time Snapshot #2: Jessica Lawton

How many kids do you have and what are their ages?

I have four children. Three girls ages 8, 7, and 3. And one little boy age 5.

How long have you been doing Morning Time?

We have been doing some form of Morning Time for about two and a half years. It began as a simple morning worship service where I helped my children practice some of the elements they could participate in at church. We would sing a hymn, read a Bible story, talk about it, and then pray.

When we began co-op classes, memory work was added to Morning Time. And finally, last year, I began to see it as the heart of our school day. I added poetry and some other read-alouds. This year, based on what I have learned about Morning Time, I have continued adding living books in more subjects, missionary stories, math stories, and puzzles. I am sure our Morning Time will continue to morph. That is half the fun!

What do you call your Morning Time?

Plain old "Morning Time." It seems a strange name, but it works. Perhaps we should have a "Name Our Morning

Time" contest with the children. That could be fun. How about "The Wonder Hour?"

Typically how long does your Morning Time take on an average day?

On an average day, our Morning Time takes about one hour.

What is your favorite Morning Time subject or activity?

I love it all! But if I had to choose, I would say our daily reading from some sort of living book. Each day I read aloud from a book on our subject of the day. I am a book collector and enjoy scouring yard sales and thrift stores for older, more conversational nonfiction. It is so much more enjoyable to read about beetles or atoms or steamboats when the book tells stories instead of dry information. This is the part of our Morning Time where I feel most like I am learning with my children, not teaching them. We are all learning from the author of the book. What amazing conversations have come from this part of our Morning Time!

What is your kids' favorite Morning Time subject or activity?

Ruth (8) says, "I really like the stories we read from the Bible and *Steamboats to the West*." Benaiah (5) says, "Reading from the Bible." Sarah Joan (7) says, "I like poetry."

What is your biggest struggle with Morning Time?

My biggest struggle is wanting to put so much into it! The world is full of amazing stuff! I struggle to remember that although I am enjoying a subject and would like to dig deeper, sometimes my kids are just done. Their little minds are happy with just a little bit. I have to remember that as an adult, I can hold more; whereas they fill up much faster.

How have you seen Morning Time bear fruit in your home?

Our Morning Worship part of Morning Time has helped my children be more involved in our church service. It is so much fun, if not slightly embarrassing, to have them yell out, just before we are about to sing a song in church, "WE KNOW THIS ONE!" We do not spend a long time in Morning Worship. It is maybe 10-15 min of our time. However, I have seen that the small stones laid consistently will build knowledge of our faith. I don't expect to change their hearts by doing this, because I can't. I only expect to do what I ought in teaching them who God is and what He has done.

I have seen an intense interest in the more academic subjects we cover in Morning Time. They love to find out about things. They love it when they notice something we have read about in a different context. They love it when I read to them. I think Morning Time is bearing the fruit of a love of learning.

What are some of your favorite Morning Time resources?

This is like asking me to pick my favorite child! For the worship part of our Morning Time, I love Terry Johnson's book, *The Family Worship Book*. It includes the why and how to begin family worship as well as the texts to many hymns and psalms to get you started.

For Morning Time in general, I think my best resource is Pam! We have had so many conversations about what to add to it and how to make it an instrument for true education. Because having a successful Morning Time is not the end goal, but rather a tool to get you to your end goal of educating a real human being. Pam is a great Morning Time resource for two reasons. One, she has written a whole book on it! But most importantly, she is a good friend who knows our family and can help hone my focus in this area. So, if Pam didn't live right up the street, I would answer that any good friend to bounce ideas off of is one of my favorite resources.

Another resource I utilize, perhaps to excess, is the thrift store. Anywhere I can go to look at and buy used, older books. More often than not, it is the best place to find living books that I never knew existed. I have a lovely conversational book about beetles by Wilfrid S. Bronson and one on the atom by Leonard de Vries.

For poetry we just LOVE *The Random House Book of Poetry for Children* by Jack Prelutsky. There are classic poems, funny poems, poems about beauty... It is just a great mix for Poetry Thursdays.

What are some of the ritual practices you include in Morning Time?

Our Morning Time looks different each day, but one thing that never changes is how we begin: always with our hymn or psalm of the month. The kids sing, clap, and sometimes play instruments. Next I read from our story Bible. Usually they beg for just one more story. Benaiah says this is his favorite part. I happen to think this is because we are reading Old Testament stories and usually someone is fighting a battle. Lastly we recite the prayer we are memorizing, and I pray for our day.

On days where Morning Time must be cut short for appointments or family commitments, I try to always squeeze in this prayer. It is that important. I want my children to remember that God comes first, and our worship of Him should be a part of our everyday lives, not just something we do on Sunday.

eight

Total Recall
— Implementing Recitation

Like so many of you, I attended public school for the first thirteen years of my education. Then after college I spent seven more years in the public school system as a teacher. It was ingrained in me that critical thinking and creativity were the pinnacle of what we wanted our students to do each day. Rote memorization and daily drill are passé in modern education. As a teacher, I was led to believe that this was because students found these practices boring and meaningless. Why should we spend time making students miserable learning something they could simply look up in a reference (or now Google)? Instead we should make education fun and exciting.

Imagine my surprise when I started doing recitation (or memory work) with my own children, and they loved it. Instead of finding it boring, they loved learning and reciting poetry because of the fun and beautiful language. Instead of being miserable, they delighted in singing the history timeline and skip counting chants. And when they come across a piece of memory work that they know in daily life? A mention of a historical name in a homily, a mathematical formula in a math lesson, or the reference to some tidbit in a book makes them joyful with their own knowledge of the subject.

A child's delight is not the only reason to incorporate recitation into your morning time, though it is one of the most satisfying ones. There are many ways recitation benefits your children.

Writing Truth on Our Hearts

My conscience is an annoying thing at times. Of course I appreciate the fact that she does a fairly good job of keeping me out of big trouble, but her tendency to nudge me about things I need to remember often comes at times when I am about to have the most fun. "Do unto others as you would have them do unto you,"[35] she whispers right about the time I am ready to deliver a juicy bit of news to a friend. "Honor your father and mother,"[36] she admonishes when even though an adult, I want to stamp my foot about something my mother has done.

Recalling these words is unavoidable, because they have been written on my heart. At some time in Sunday School past, these verses were ones I memorized. Not only have they never left me, they still guide my daily actions (most of the time). Memorizing truth from Scripture is one way to be always guided by right thinking. (Acting on it is much harder—I will leave that discussion to better authors than I.)

The Importance of Forms

In her delightful talk "Memorization and the Soul: Why, What, and How," Brandy Vencel tells us that Frederick Douglass was a great orator because he used memorized speeches as a basis for writing his own. While the words and ideas were his, the forms of his speeches were based on those of some of the most famous speeches from history.[37] When we memorize, we are not only memorizing the content of poems, stories, and speeches, but we are also internalizing the structures of these genres as well. Once we are familiar with the forms, we are then able to transfer our own words and meaning into those forms and use them for our individual expression.

Fodder for Contemplation

Andrew Pudewa reminds us in his talk "Nurturing Competent Communicators" that you cannot get anything out of a brain that has nothing in it to begin with.[38] If a student is going to be able to write, speak, and express himself, then he must have something in his mind to use for that purpose. By filling our students' heads with beautiful words, great literature, historical tidbits, and wonderful quotes, we give them a basis for writing essays and compositions. With a mind full of Scripture, quotes, and beautiful poetry, we can never be bored—even without a book, we will always have something to think about, consider, and mull over.

Warning: Low Memory

Sadly, our short-term memory only has limited space for information and processing. This is why we can't remember the grocery list once we get to the store, unless we have written it down. Our limited short-term memory has jettisoned that information for new pieces by the time we get there.

Memorizing moves information to long-term memory where the storage space is much larger, and there it can stay until we need it. This is why the nemesis of most fifth graders is long division. This is not because long division is so terribly complicated, but instead it is because this is the very first time a student must use all four operations—addition, subtraction, multiplication, and division—in order to solve one problem. That's quite a few processes going on in the brain at one time. Students with instant recall of their math facts struggle much less, if at all. Students without the facts memorized have to use up valuable short-term memory space remembering facts instead of remembering processes for long division. Is it any wonder that they struggle so?

What Then Should We Memorize?

The first question I get about memorization and recitation is always, "What should we spend our time memorizing?" The answer depends on your educational goals and practices. Some families will focus exclusively on Scripture, while at the other end of the spectrum some families will have an entire litany of memory work they learn. In our family we choose to memorize facts and also what I call heart-work—

Scripture, poems, prayers, Shakespeare. We approach each set differently. The facts are learned with our co-op and practiced in the year they are being learned. For most subjects, that means new sets of facts every year for four years, though we do repeat some things like our history timeline and math facts annually. Then these facts are put aside and not reviewed again until they come up again in the cycle.

For most of these facts, we are looking to build a peg instead of total recall, though it is likely we will achieve recall once my kids have been through a couple of cycles of this memory work. On the other hand, we learn the heart-work at a much slower pace. We begin with a smaller body, slowly add additional pieces, and take the time to let it shape us. In our family we make the time to study both kinds of memory work, but we take the time to internalize the latter.

My thoughts and ideas on memory work and recitation have changed greatly over the past three years and are still changing as I learn and observe my own kids. I am doing what is best for us, and you should do the same. Memorization questions can be a point of contention among homeschoolers, with different viewpoints and methods claiming to be the better path.

I would encourage you to rise above the fray and do exactly what is best for your family. You are only limited by time. You must have the time to memorize everything you undertake. Evaluate each piece of memory work you add to your repertoire and decide if it is worth the time you will need to devote to it.

Some ideas for memory work include:

- Scripture

- Poetry

- Shakespeare

- Prayers in English and Latin

- Math facts, formulas, and laws

- History timeline

- Latin grammar chants

- Grammar rules and parts of speech

- Catechism

- Excerpts from speeches and historical documents

- Science facts

- History facts

How to Memorize

Memory work and recitation do not have to be dry and boring. If they are, then you need to change the way you are doing them. Here are a few of my best tips for learning new memory work.

Start with one thing to memorize. If your children are totally new to recitation, then a poem—preferably a short and humorous one—is a fabulous place to start. The easiest way to start memorizing is to simply read a line to your children and have them repeat it back to you. If your children are old enough to read, you can certainly provide them with their own printed copy of the material; but that is not necessary. Choose a selection that is about five or six words long and then have them repeat. Do this with maybe two six-word sections and stop for the day. For example, if memorizing "Stopping By Woods on A Snowy Evening," on day one you would open your binder and read: "Whose woods these are I think I know." Your children would then repeat that line. Then you would recite: "His house is in the village, though."[39] Again they would repeat. Then you would read the first line again and wait for a repeat. Then read the second line again and repeat. Close your book and you are done for the day. How easy is that?

The next day you would do the same thing again and close the book. By day three there is a pretty good chance that when you start reading the first line, some earnest youngster is going to start reciting it with you. This is a good thing, so let them do it! Still say the line twice and make sure everyone is saying the second repetition with you. On this day, you can add one or two more lines to your stanza. As you continue, each day add a line or two, until before long everyone will be able to recite the entire poem. Remember, the repeat method is only used when you are learning a new piece. Once the piece is learned and moved to review, then you will just say the piece aloud and the children will join in with you.

When my kids and I first started this method, there was a bit of resistance to it. The problem was not that they didn't like to memorize, but that they felt like I was quizzing them all of the time. This is why I let the kids say the first line with me if they want, and I always repeat the line with them. I am a fellow student in this matter—not a quizzing mom. Who likes to be put on the spot every single day? Not I, and I shouldn't expect my kids to be any different. Now there usually comes a time when someone announces, "I can do this one myself." In that case I let them take pride in that accomplishment. And on occasion I will ask one student to recite a piece or part of a piece alone, but this happens about once weekly, not every single day.

While the recite and repeat method is the easiest way to learn memory work, we have a few other methods that we enjoy for our review. If you have someone who likes to see the written text better, you can provide them with printed copies that have a picture to help connect the memory work to a visual cue. The moms in our homeschool co-op get together for a work day each year to make a set of Powerpoint slides for each week of our memory work. We use them in the co-op to present the memory work, but families can use them at home as well, displaying them on a computer or tablet.

Other students will greatly enjoy setting the memory work to music and singing it. My children like this quite a bit, so sometimes I take the time to set some facts to song. I sing the memory work into an app on my phone that creates an MP3 that I can then put into a playlist in iTunes. I create playlists (of my own recordings and purchased memory work recordings) of musical and spoken versions of memory work. When it is time to review, I only have to hit play.

Some memory work better lends itself to a chant or cheer instead of a song. The kids love to set their memory work to hand motions and cheerlead some pieces in unison. Some days we also play games to review our memory work.

A laundry basket and a rolled pair of socks make a fun "basketball" game—you get a shot when you recite a piece correctly. *Connect Four* and *Jenga* also lend themselves well to memory-work play. There are many days that I simply want to sit, recite, and be done with memory work quickly, but the days when we add a bit of spice to our recitation are the ones the children enjoy most.

My friend and fellow homeschool mom Ann Karako's favorite way to memorize with the kids is to write the entire passage on a chalkboard or whiteboard and then read it aloud as a group over and over again, erasing one word with each subsequent reading. So the next time the kids read the passage, they have to provide the word to fill in the blank. She chooses words that are separated from one another to start, then gradually the blanks start to be close together or consecutive. This can be done over several days if it is a long passage. It is very effective and also quite painless. With small kids who can't yet read, each word can be placed on a separate index card, taped to the refrigerator, and written in a different color. They would repeat each word after the teacher until they got to the blank where she had removed an index card, then she would help them with the word at first until they could provide it without prompting. Then they would remove another index card and repeat the process.

Most of the time we are working on memory work, my children are doing something else with their hands—drawing, coloring, and play dough are some favorite activities. Our family rule is that your mouth has to be moving during memory work. For most people, simply listening to a piece will not put it in memory, but reciting the piece will make sure it is stored where it can be recalled. That said, there is much singing, motion, and creativity during our morning recitation sessions, which make it a much-anticipated part of the school day.

You probably don't need me to tell you that if you learn a piece but do not recite it again, then you won't remember it six months later. In order to keep these items in our memory long-term, they will need to be periodically reviewed. There are a number of different systems or methods out there for reviewing old memory work. You will need to strike a balance between which method is most effective for you and which you have time to complete each day.

In his program *Linguistic Development Through Poetry Memorization*, Andrew Pudewa outlines a memorization system built upon the Suzuki Music Method. In the system you gradually learn poems, and all new and review poems are reviewed every day. After a set of about 20 poems is learned, you begin on a new set of poems. All poems in set two are reviewed every day while poems from set one are then reviewed only every other day. Yes, it is a ton of review. Yes, you will never forget any of these poems. And even though the system is written for poems it could be used for any memory work.[40]

Simply Charlotte Mason has a Scripture Memory System that can be used for Scripture and other pieces of memory work. New pieces are recited daily and then moved through a series of lessening review—every other day, to once a week, to once a month. A video on their website outlines how to set up the review system.[41] Once again, they use it for Scripture, but it can be adapted for any kind of memory work. I have also adapted the system to use with a binder instead of a card file. I am much too lazy to copy all of our memory work on cards but prefer to print it out on the computer instead.

With the *Simply Charlotte Mason* system you may have less to review per day than with Pudewa's method, but after a year or so you will still have a large amount of memory work to review on a regular basis. Mystie Winckler of *Simply Convivial* has adapted the system to include even fewer review days. She makes up for the fewer review slots by rotating out memory work in a block schedule. She has a set that is reviewed every week the first term of the year. That set is then replaced for the second six-week term by another set of memory work to review.[42] Each term sees a new set of memory work come back into the binder for review. This means that her family keeps old memory work from previous years in a review rotation, but not as often as the other systems.

This raises the question—how perfectly should memory work be recalled? What we as the parent-teachers must remember, however, is that we can't control our child's memory or mind. What they remember in one year or ten is less our responsibility than the fact that we gave them the time and the relationship with the material to form connections. Mostly we try our best and we remember that this process takes time. We are not doing recitation to earn a prize, check off a box, or perform for grandma. We are doing it to allow what we memorize to change us from within or to use what we learn as a tool to make future learning easier. This means we commit to learning things that are the best and to spending the years it takes to learn it well without rushing through.

Morning Time Snapshot #3: Bethany Barendregt

How many kids do you have and what are their ages?

I have five kids: three boys and two girls, in that order. Our boys are 9, 7, and 5. The girls are busy toddlers, ages 3 and 10 months. (I count the 10-month-old as a toddler now because she walks and gets into everything.)

How long have you been doing Morning Time?

I've been doing some kind of morning devotional with our children since my oldest was a toddler. It's always included Scripture and often catechism and memory work. For our entire homeschooling experience, I've either been pregnant or had a baby, so our time together has looked different depending on which stage we are in at the moment. We've worked on memorizing passages or single verses in Scripture, and we would often move from Bible reading or stories into literature books or poetry.

In 2015, when I was introduced to Sarah Mackenzie's blog, I found out that what I was doing was called Morning Time, which led me to begin really looking at ways to make our time together take a more intentional shape. I devoured podcasts and written materials, trying to discover the best way to bless our family with this tool, and now we've been doing Morning Time in a structured way for about a year and a half.

What do you call your Morning Time?

Most of the time I call it Morning Time. However, I have a very rebellious brain that doesn't like calling something "Morning Time" if we're doing it at lunchtime, so I'm still looking for a clever name to work with. I know some people call it "Symposium" if they're doing it in the afternoon, but I've spent too much time trying to explain that name to my smaller children. So for now, I stick with Morning Time regardless of what time it happens.

Typically how long does your Morning Time take on an average day?

It depends on the day, but it ranges anywhere between 20 minutes to an hour.

Our Mondays are very busy with online classes and boys' choir, so I try to squeeze in a decent 20-minute Morning Time routine. We actually do Morning Time in the car on Tuesday morning, which involves everything I can do while driving and lasts around 20 minutes.

Wednesday through Friday, our Morning Time is around an hour in length and involves longer readings or activities. Even on the days when our Morning Time is shorter, I am thankful for the routine and joy that our rituals bring to our day.

What is your favorite Morning Time subject or activity?

That's a hard one to answer! I really love singing with my children; but I think if I had to pick one activity, I would stick with Scripture reading and Bible memory work.

The year our youngest was born was the hardest year of my mothering life so far, and it was the regular, daily Bible reading and memorization with the kids that really got me through the toughest days. I wanted to make sure, if nothing else happened during Morning Time, that I provided my kids with passages to fill their souls with goodness. We memorized key passages like 1 John 1, Psalm 23, 1 Corinthians 13, Philippians 2, and 1 Timothy 6:6-12.

I had started out with a desire to give my children "tools" to keep in their lives, especially for times of discouragement or moments when we needed to remember the right way to treat each other. In the end, I ended up being immensely blessed by memorizing the passages along with them! We also saw so much fruit and growth in our boys from the discussions we had about how to apply the passages to our lives.

What is your kids' favorite Morning Time subject or activity?

They love singing and memory work challenges. But I think their favorite activity would be when I pick out a book and read aloud, and they get to draw a picture of what I'm reading. I try to encourage them to just enjoy drawing or coloring while I read and not worry about perfectly illustrating. I'm not particularly artsy, so it's been great to see them feel the freedom to branch out beyond what I would naturally tend to do. As a result, I have some really fun illustrations collected of different drawings they've done—the Globe Theatre, Shakespeare's life and home, Shakespearean plays, Erik the Red, and some Viking ships, to name a few from this past school year.

What is your biggest struggle with Morning Time?

Other than keeping my toddler and baby happy (and occupied safely), I think my biggest struggle would be choosing to remember that we are not wasting time by doing Morning Time, nor am I a failure at Morning Time if we have to pause to take care of an issue or stop earlier than I had planned. I have a tendency to be very task-oriented; and if I start to think, "I'm wasting time by doing Morning Time when I have X to do, or we need to accomplish X," then I know I'm missing the point of what that time is set aside for. And if I end up thinking that way, then the solution for me is to remind myself that homeschooling is about relationship. I have to keep front and center that I'm building something lasting in my children by investing in these moments.

We have a saying at our house that what you practice is what you will become. Most of the time, when we use this statement, it has to do with someone's behavior or attitude, but I think that it really is my mantra when it comes to Morning Time, as well. My goal with Morning Time, ultimately, is for our family to practice loveliness and become lovely.

How have you seen Morning Time bear fruit in your home?

Our relationships with our boys have really deepened as we've started to have meaningful discussions about different subjects. I like to think we all enjoy each other more now than we did two years ago. Part of that is their growing maturity, I know, but I do believe that a big part of it is that I'm not just focused on checking off a list of duties. We're cultivating a love of learning, collecting tools for life, and deepening our relationships because of what we are choosing to fill our lives with.

My husband and I are also seeing our boys grow in their enjoyment of learning new concepts and meeting challenges as opportunities, not roadblocks to be feared. I'm really enjoying passing on my love of subjects like Shakespeare and art history. Watching their excitement over these new worlds has been such a beautiful thing, and I feel so privileged to be able to witness it first-hand!

What are some of your favorite Morning Time resources?

Oh dear, where to start? I try to choose our resources keeping in mind that we are in the business of growing people with souls and minds. I do have a limited amount of time right now before boys get antsy and my toddler girls get into something or become grumpy.

For the faith portion of our Morning Time, some of our favorite resources we've used are:

- *The Cantus Christi Hymnal* (or an online hymn resource to print off our hymn of the month)

- The book *Hidden Treasures* by Pam Forster

- *Egermeier's Story Bible*

- *The Biggest Story* by Kevin DeYoung or *The Big Picture Story Bible* by David Helm—both well-written and engaging Bible story books.

For our read-aloud time:

Our read-alouds are focused on history, poetry, and fables or fairy tales. I am a bit of a book collector/hoarder, but I love having the option to choose read-alouds from something we have on the bookshelf. We love the *Beautiful Feet Books* options for historical biographies! I also think *Usborne Books* has some really wonderful options for history and science, as well as fables, stories from Shakespeare, and fairy tales.

I love using the online library catalog to locate books that are recommended from sources like *Exodus Books* and the *Read Aloud Revival*. We also have a few beautifully-illustrated poetry books and Mother Goose books that my children adore!

Other book resources we have enjoyed in the past:

- *Draw Europe* by Kristin Draeger

- *Maps* by Aleksandra Mizielinska

- *Life Science* DVDs

- *Nature Anatomy* by Julia Rothman

- *Dover* Coloring Books

- Bruce Colville's illustrated Shakespeare stories

- *Mad Libs* (a huge favorite, and often requested on car rides)

Some more favorite "resources" are the things I use to make sure Morning Time runs smoothly. The most important is my cup of coffee! Helpful tools include:

- Cookies, muffins, or granola bars (really any snack that keeps people at the table)

- M&M's for memory work rewards/incentives

- Magnetic "paper" dolls for my three-year-old to play with to keep her happy and out of trouble.

I also put together a set of "busy boxes": shoebox-size, clear totes labeled with days of the week that I've collected different activities in. They're a bit scrambled now (because, well, toddlers...), but they mostly contain toddler-safe puzzles, magnetic letters, magnetic animals, and a magnetic board.

Note: at one point, I tried using sticker books to keep my toddler busy, but that ended up being too labor-intensive for me, because if I wasn't paying attention, I was rewarded with Disney Princesses stuck to every available surface.

Last, my favorite resource is freedom! If we need to go to an appointment, we can cut Morning Time short or do it in the car. If we didn't manage to get to the read-aloud portion of our day, we can listen to an audiobook or one of my older boys can read aloud in the car. The important thing is that we are together, not where we are seated or how much we got done.

What are some of the ritual practices you include in Morning Time?

We have a core of daily Morning Time work that we add to, depending on the day. This involves starting with the Doxology or Sanctus, taking turns praying together, singing our hymn of the month, and reading a short devotional or Bible passage before we work on our Scripture memory work. (At this point, I usually dismiss my toddler to go play or pull out something for her to play with, if I think she would enjoy the read-aloud without being too disruptive.)

Then we do our read-aloud, and after this, we typically start on our memory work for Classical Conversations. Wednesdays through Fridays, we incorporate an additional subject such as Geography, Art, Science, or Shakespeare, depending on the term we are in. It might appear from my list of favorite resources that our load is heavy and intense, but I really just pick one extra subject to do per day in addition to our core.

nine

Planning a Morning Time

Homeschool planning is one of my very favorite things to do. I think this is because everything is just so perfect in a good plan. Once the execution starts, then a good planner has to dodge, feint, and adapt to meet reality; but for a brief, shining moment when I close my planning book, all is right with the world.

I do myself and my children a great disservice, though, if I don't try to plan things that meet our reality from the very beginning; so over the years I have gotten better and better at doing just that. A Morning Time plan grounded in reality is going to be your greatest ally in making the practice work from the very beginning. Let's look at ways we can strike a balance between the pastoral imaginings of Morning Time that you might be enjoying in your head and the reality of your schedule and your children.

The place to begin when planning your first Morning Time is with the concept of a ramp-up. I really can't stress this enough. Very few people can birth a fully grown Morning Time full of rich activities from the start and expect to be able to execute it perfectly. Instead, start with one or two small

Morning Time practices—prayer and a hymn are a lovely place to begin. Do those practices for a couple of weeks and then add one more practice. Maybe it will be a bit of Scripture reading or a chapter from a great book. After another week, you might then add something else, continuing with this practice until your Morning Time has taken the form that you desire. Small, successful practices will bear more fruit than overwhelming plans that do not get done.

Once you have passed the ramp-up phase, and Morning Time has become a habit in your home, you might get excited about making your plans more elaborate. (Note: you don't have to. Continuing to do exactly what you have been doing is a worthy endeavor for the long haul.) First, make a list of the subjects that you would like to include during your Morning Time. Start with the 3 Rs—ritual, reading aloud, and recitation—and then refer to Chapter Ten for other subject ideas. At this point you are only listing the subjects you would like to do, the resources you would like to use, and how much time each piece will take.

Now that you have your wish list of subjects, you can begin to plug them into a daily schedule. Because a plan with more subjects will take more time, you will likely not do every subject every single day and will need to decide what will be done when. In my current plan, prayer and recitation are the only things done daily. Other subjects—like hymn study, music appreciation, and nature study—are only done one or two days a week.

We only do Morning Time four days each week. This is because we have co-op each Tuesday. Getting out the door to co-op is difficult enough, so I do not try to do Morning Time on those days. Also, we have homeschool karate each

Thursday at 1:00 PM. This means that we need to be done with school by noon so we can have lunch and be on time. I purposefully keep Morning Time a bit shorter on that day by doing fewer subjects and subjects that take less time. I have adapted my Morning Time schedule and expectations to work with the reality of our schedule.

Using Block and Loop Scheduling with Morning Time

One way you can fit more subjects into your Morning Time is by using block scheduling, for which the possibilities are limitless. One easy way is to set up your school year in five- or six-week terms. Each term you change out the subjects you will do in your Morning Time. Let's say you want to block the fine arts subjects. One term you might do music appreciation, the next might be drawing instruction, then picture study; then you can repeat each block. Your terms can also be semester-length to stick with a single subject for a longer period of time.

For example we might do music appreciation studies for 20 weeks. After those 20 weeks are up, we will use that same slot in the schedule to do Shakespeare for the next 16 weeks. It just conveniently happened that the resources I wanted to use for both of those subjects were easily adapted to the schedule I needed.

Loop scheduling can also be beneficial for Morning Time. Loop scheduling means not assigning specific subjects to specific days, but instead working from a list and simply doing the next thing each day. Once you have worked through the entire list, you simply start at the beginning again. This works well when you get stressed out about missing specific days and the subjects planned for those days.

So let's say you do prayer and recitation each day. The rest of your Morning Time subjects could happen on a loop—maybe history read-aloud, picture study, music appreciation, drawing practice, and poetry. You set aside an hour and fifteen minutes each day for Morning Time. After prayer and recitation, you start with history read-aloud. That day you might get to two or three things on your list before time runs out. The next day you start again with prayer and recitation, and pick up on the loop list where you left off. Repeat each day. Because subjects are not assigned to specific days, there is no stress when a day is missed. You simply pick up the next day where you left off.

You can also use a loop schedule to loop content within a subject. For example, maybe you want to have one read-aloud session during Morning Time. You can loop books between science or math biography, historical fiction, classic tale, poetry, or Shakespeare. Every day during that reading session you will pick up the next book and read a section from it. In our schedule we have a spot three days a week for "Religious Reading." We read a bit of the Gospel each day during morning prayers, but I also want to carve out time to read Bible stories, saint stories, and catechism stories or allegory. I have three books I have chosen to read (see Chapter 10). During "Religious Reading" time, I simply choose the next book in line and read a bit from it for the day.

The most important thing is to create a Morning Time schedule that will work for your family. There really is no wrong way to do it. My friend Jessica has a Morning Time schedule three days a week. Then on the fourth day her family does prayer and poetry. They see it as a welcome weekly break from the Morning Time routine. It works for her family, so it is good.

Organizing Materials

Organization is not about pretty (though pretty is not at all a bad thing). Organization is about preparedness. It is the tool that helps you make sure the job gets done. If I sit down to do Morning Time and I don't have my plans, or books, or supplies, or printed papers—whatever it is I need—ready and at hand, it interrupts the flow of what I am doing, often to the extent that whatever is missing just doesn't get done.

I always pull out my *Plan Your Year* homeschool planner and begin planning the school year weeks ahead of time in the summer. I like to get everything mapped out on paper and then gather my supplies together for the entire year in one place. Friends sometimes question the amount of work and effort that I put into planning. While I do enjoy the process, more importantly I enjoy the fact that once I am in the heat of the school year, and fatigue has set in on so many fronts, I can simply open up my plans and do the next thing. I plan extensively ahead of time, thinking everything through while the kids are enjoying their summer, so I don't have to think nearly as much when the school year is upon us.

The same goes for my Morning Time plan. With the plan in hand, the next task is to pull all the materials I will need and have them ready to use. I do this using a double-tiered organization method. First, I have a shelf on my bookshelf set aside for all the materials that will be used this year. Books and other items can be stored together on that shelf right near my workspace, within easy reach throughout the year. In addition to that space, I also keep a Morning Time basket for all the current Morning Time supplies. This includes books, student binders, maps, CDs or DVDs, etc. I switch out the supplies when we finish a resource.

Does your container have to be a basket? Not at all. I just happen to like mine because it has sloped sides, holds everything I need, and fits neatly in my shelf cube. Your Morning Time container could be a plastic bin, shelf, or even a tote bag if you tend to pick up and do Morning Time elsewhere. Do what works best for you, and by all means use what you have on hand when you can. The most important thing is that everything you need is stored right there together.

The next component of my Morning Time organization system is my Morning Time binder. I use a variation of the *Simply Charlotte Mason* system[43] that I outlined in the recitation chapter. The binder is divided into a number of sections, with the first being a spot for my plans and form printouts. This is where I keep the record of what we will be doing in Morning Time for the year, including the plan for the year, the weekly schedule, and any loop schedule lists I might have made.

Next is the section for our Morning Time procedures. This is where I keep the procedure lists I have made for subjects that don't have a set curriculum. These procedures outline step-by-step what we should do when we sit down to do a specific subject. They keep me from having to think and remember what comes next, and they make my Morning

Time open-and-go. I set up all of these procedures in the summer for the following year.

Here is an example for studying *Story of the World*, a history text for elementary kids we have used in our Morning Time.

1. Write names and place names from chapter on whiteboard.

2. Listen to chapter while completing coloring page.

3. Provide oral narration of part of chapter. Use questions and names on whiteboard as needed.

4. Look up topic in *Usborne Encyclopedia of World History*. View any interesting internet links.

5. Complete map work.

Story of the World is a great resource. It even has a wonderful activity book, which is full of so much information and so many things to make and do. I get a little overwhelmed by it all. So I made my own list of what I wanted to do each time we study a *Story of the World* chapter. It took just a few minutes to come up with the plan, decide on the resources to use, and type up the list on a paper.

That paper then goes into my Morning Time binder, and I refer to it until the procedure becomes second-nature to me to follow. I also print out all of the coloring pages and map pages I will need ahead of time and store them in a folder.

If I waited to print until we needed them, they would never get printed.

Next comes the memory-work section that includes the series of tabs for our memory work progression. We use a daily tab and also one each for Monday, Wednesday, Thursday, and Friday (we have co-op on Tuesdays). Here is what is under each tab:

- Daily tab: Our current week's memory work from co-op

- Monday: science/math/review (one or two older pieces of memory work)

- Wednesday: Latin/review

- Thursday: great words/review

- Friday: grammar/geography/review

The final section of the binder includes the remainder of the memory work we will use that year—printed, placed in page protectors, and sorted so I can easily find what I need. Some moms also create a binder for each of their children so they can read along with the memory work.

Another vital part of my organization process is getting all of my playlists in order for the year. In the past I have created my playlists in iTunes and then moved playlists back and forth off my iPhone when I needed them. Since now we have an Amazon Prime account, I am going to try storing my memory work playlists on the cloud instead, to save room on my phone. I will then be able to access them from my Kindle or iPhone through the Amazon music app. My friend Jessica plays her songs from folders on Google Drive using her Android tablet.

There are any number of ways to store and play your music. You will just need to seek out online tutorials that walk you through the process for your particular device and your chosen app. The most important thing is to use a folder system or playlist to organize your music by week, term, or topic before you need it.

As you can see, Morning Time planning and organizing is not rocket science. The most important take-aways are to start slow, decide what you want to do, and then be sure to gather everything you need ahead of time, having it together in one spot and handy for when you need it. This makes it much more likely that Morning Time will happen when the time comes.

Morning Time Snapshot #4: Kara Anderson

How many kids do you have and what are their ages?

I have two kids—newly 10 and newly 13, which makes me feel a bit like we're entering a new phase of Morning Time together! In many ways, it's more fun, because Morning Time gives us a chance to talk; and I'm seeing their personalities and opinions emerge so much—they're really interesting people!

How long have you been doing Morning Time?

We are newer to Morning Time. It's our third year. We used to do something called Circle Time when the kids were younger, which had some similarities.

Circle Time is based on Waldorf tradition, which is one of the learning philosophies that influenced us a lot in the early years. Transitioning to Morning Time has been great for us as the kids have grown up!

What do you call your Morning Time?

"School." Isn't that boring? I wish it had a fun name, but because we also draw from unschooling philosophy, we don't have definitive distinctions to our learning during the day. So after breakfast, we start "school," which means gathering around the table and going through our Morning

Basket materials together; then we'll break off for individual projects, reading, independent study, etc.

Typically how long does your Morning Time take on an average day?

It's between 30 and 60 minutes, depending on what else we have going on that day and attention spans. I recently participated in a class with Mystie Winckler about homeschooling personalities, and I learned such a big key— as an INFJ, I am really strongly influenced by how my kids are feeling on a given day. (This has seriously been life-changing for me.)

So sometimes, I will make the choice to keep our Morning Time a bit shorter so that we can get to independent "free-choice" work sooner.

The truth is, things just don't work here when I push— the kids are NOT learning, I am stressed, and everyone is miserable.

That class has given me permission to intentionally keep things short or even (gasp!) skip Morning Time if it's a really rough morning.

What is your favorite Morning Time subject or activity?

I LOVE picture study. I totally didn't see this coming. But we get the picture-study packets from *Simply Charlotte Mason*, and they are so well done! I loved studying art in college, and it's so fun to learn about artists with my kids NOW. I love that they don't have to wait until they are 20 to learn this stuff!

What is your kids' favorite Morning Time subject or activity?

Math and Logic! Lately, we've been laughing a lot over *Life of Fred Math*. It's just so ridiculous, and it's so short—my kids love Fred. I've been trying to be more hands-on with math too, sometimes using candy as manipulatives, or math games.

Math isn't a natural favorite for any of us, so I'm definitely employing a spoonful-of-sugar philosophy here!

What is your biggest struggle with Morning Time?

Just getting going. I joke that sometimes I have to filibuster. I just have to start talking (reading!). Once we get going, it's all good.

How have you seen Morning Time bear fruit in your home?

My kids think Shakespeare is funny! They recognize Monet in the doctor's office! They understand Latin roots, so when we went to the science museum and did a DNA class, they could figure what many of the scientific words meant.

What are some of your favorite Morning Time resources?

- *Picture Study Portfolios* from *Simply Charlotte Mason*

- The D'Aulaires' books. We finished *Greek Myths* earlier this year and we're working on *Norse Myths*

- *Life of Fred*

- *Classics to Read Aloud to Your Children,* edited by William F. Russell

- Leon Garfield's *Shakespeare Stories*

- *The Fallacy Detective*

- Shel Silverstein poetry collections

- Pearler beads! (These have been HUGE this year in helping to keep hands busy while we learn).

What are some of the ritual practices you include in Morning Time?

We always light a candle at the start and blow it out at the end—again, this is left over from Circle Time.

We always use our "notebooks"—these are large, artists' notebooks that the kids can use for drawing (while they are listening), doodling, or taking notes. These aren't notebooks for the state or to show the grandparents; they are just a way to avoid paper clutter while giving the kids something to do with their hands as they listen.

Ten

Put This in Your Basket

I have never been to a feast, but I have been to a few buffets. A few years ago, when the kids were much younger, my family had dinner (southern dinner—the noon meal) at a quaint little restaurant in Georgia. The restaurant was in an old house with a maze of downstairs rooms. The atmosphere was unique, but the food was divine. The buffet had chicken (fried, of course), roast, fish, meatloaf, mashed potatoes, rice, gravies (white and brown), fried green tomatoes, fried okra, and any number of vegetables seasoned with bacon drippings (yum, scout's honor). For dessert there was banana pudding and red velvet cake. As a diner I could have gone and selected a good portion of a few things, but most likely I nibbled at many, enjoying the food I love but never have time to make at home.

Now that I am salivating, I can explain that Morning Time subjects are much like that buffet. There are a wide variety of subjects that you can place in your morning basket—all of them very good. Sure, there are some things to take into consideration when choosing subjects to include in your Morning Time, but there are very few wrong answers to the question. You can choose to go deeper with a few subjects or to sample small portions of many.

Consider that Cindy Rollins says that MorningTime is

> "the daily collection of little grains of sand that add up to a lifetime of learning. It is the daily sowing of the seeds of learning for the long haul... Over the years, MT has kept the same structure, but it can also be fluid as to categories. I think it is a great place to put all those categories which fall outside the usual school routine: composer study, artists, Plutarch, and Shakespeare; even nature notebooks are each perfect for MT, because these are the important things that often get squeezed out of the traditional school day. We may even find when we scoot over just a couple minutes a day to make room for these easily neglected areas, the connections the mind begins to make start circuits for our children which far surpass the mundane teaching of subjects."[44]

As you choose a course of study for your own Morning Time, the following five characteristics will help you make your choices:

- Is it a subject that can be done in a short amount of time—say 5-20 minutes?

- Is it a subject that your entire family (or most of them) can experience together?

- Is it a subject that you want to do, but doesn't fit in your normal school routine—something you have struggled to place in a regular spot for a while?

- Is it a subject best studied in community with opportunity for discussion?

- Is it something that you enjoy?

That last one might come as a surprise to you, but I find that it is often the most important. Without that enjoyment factor for the kids and for mom, then Morning Time becomes simply one more thing to cross off the list in the course of the school day.

Consider this advice from Sarah Mackenzie: "Make absolutely certain that you have things in Morning Time that light you on fire. So don't just put things in Morning Time that you think you should be doing; don't just put things in Morning Time that you feel guilty that you're not getting to. Put those in there; that's good, but also make sure that at least one thing every day is something that you're doing just for the sheer joy of it."[45]

If you hate teaching art or music appreciation, then cross it off the list. Outsource nature study or beautiful math if the thought of them makes you want to pluck your eyebrows instead. I do believe that you (and the kids) should give things a try that you don't think you would enjoy, but if everyone has given it a good honest go, and and no one is enjoying a subject, then let it go. We don't need Morning Time martyrs.

I will remind you that Morning Time does not have to be elaborate or full of many subjects to be rewarding, but for families who are in a season where they are able to spread a wide feast, consider some of the following subjects.

For an updated collection of clickable links to all of the following resources, visit pambarnhill.com/morningtime resources.

Fine Arts

Fine Arts subjects often get put aside in the homeschool curriculum when crunched for time. They are a wonderful candidate to include in Morning Time one or two days a week.

Music Appreciation

Choose one composer or period of music and study it for a specific term. This can be done easily in about 15-20 minutes a week. You might choose a composer like Mozart and read a picture book or biography one day a week during Morning Time. Then grab a CD (or download an album) and listen to the music of Mozart while reading, throughout the week at meals, and/or in the car. Do this for six to twelve weeks— it really is that easy. Here are some of my favorite music resources:

- *SQUILT*—Broken up by musical period, *SQUILT* provides a simple but comprehensive plan for music appreciation. Mary Prather lays out a procedure for you to follow that teaches your children the grammar of music and allows them to apply the knowledge of that grammar to various pieces. There are ten lessons per volume, but the lessons are rich enough to be stretched over two-to-three-week sessions if you add a composer biography.

- ***Getting to Know the World's Greatest Composers* by Mike Venezia**—These short picture-book biographies are easily read in one sitting and give a delightful overview of the composers' lives. Illustrated with period art, photographs, and the author's own comical drawings, they are kid favorites.

- ***Famous Children Series***—The *Famous Children Series* by *Fun with Music* tells about the childhood of famous composers. Kids can see that these famous musicians had some of the same childhood struggles they themselves have. Very relatable.

- **Composer Biographies by Opal Wheeler**—This series of composer biographies is composed of wonderful living books about the lives of various composers. These are chapter books which will need to be read in multiple sittings. My kids really enjoy these.

- ***Classics for Kids***—A free podcast resource that sorts composers by name, time period, timeline, and geographical location. There is an abundance of resources available on the site, including printable worksheets and lesson plans that could be adapted for home use, if you desire. Many composers have been featured on multiple shows, so a multi-week study of a composer could consist of listening to a series of shows about that composer.

Picture Study/Art Appreciation

Charlotte-Mason-style picture study hinges upon an oral narration of a particular artist's works. Students are told the artist's name and shown a print. They are asked to study it for a number of minutes in silence. After the allotted time, the picture is turned over; and students narrate, or tell orally, everything they can remember about the picture. The picture is then shown again and more details are discussed. As with composers, it is best to study one artist per term—for about six weeks—until the student becomes familiar with the artist's style. During this term, the artist's works could be displayed in the schoolroom or home. A biography of the artist can also be read.

- *Picture Study Portfolios*—These portfolios available from *Simply Charlotte Mason* are a complete picture-study resource. Each portfolio contains biographical information, eight works from each artist including discussion points, as well as information about the Charlotte Mason method of picture study. While there is a digital version of the product, I highly recommend the printed version with the artwork reproduced on glossy 8.5x11 cardstock.

- *Harmony Fine Arts*—This digital resource is divided into grade level and historical period (note: I combine my kids into a single grade level). You study a single artist for a period of six weeks. It includes links to the art online plus three levels of involvement—picture study only; an intermediate level with picture study, artist biography, and simple art reproduction activities; and a more complex level that includes all the others plus a hands-on art component. Composer study is also included. You will need a few extra resources, depending on which level you choose; but links to artist and composer works are provided.

- **Mike Venezia's Artist Biographies**—Like his composer series, Venezia also has a series on artists.

- *Usborne* **Art Books**—No one does art books better than *Usborne*. For the simplest picture study of all, grab the *Usborne Book of Famous Paintings* and simply study one spread per week, discussing each one. We also love the *Usborne Book of Famous Artists* and the *Sticker Book of Famous Artists*. Some of the books are internet-linked, which means *Usborne* curates a kid-safe webpage with links to websites with more information.

Art and Handicrafts

While I don't tend to pull out a large amount of art supplies and do in-depth instruction during Morning Time, we do sometimes do simple drawing or watercolor projects. Morning Time would also be a perfect time to learn to crochet a chain or knit a scarf. (I have been known to knit during memory-work recitation or audio-book read-alouds myself.) Here are a few simple resources you might use:

- *Drawing Textbook* **by Bruce McIntyre**—This simple little book (more of a thick pamphlet) is a wonderful series of lessons on learning to draw with perspective, shape, and shading. There are thirty-seven lessons and 222 exercises. These are perfect for practicing drawing skills during Morning Time.

- *Chalkpastel.com*—This site, run by homeschooling mom Tricia Hodges and her mother Lucia "Nana" Hames, has handy little eBooks and video tutorials which are a fun way to incorporate some simple art into your Morning Time. Not at all fussy, you can simply read the brief tutorial or show the video of Nana leading art class, and your kids can create wonderful works while you read aloud or do recitation. Yes, the pastels do make a small mess; but having a pack of baby wipes handy is the key for a successful chalk pastels session.

- **Watercolor Pencils**—We don't have a specific resource we use to teach us technique, but we do love watercolor pencils. The kids create with them and simply add water for blending.

- ***Simply Charlotte Mason Handicrafts Made Simple DVDs***—These DVDs of five different handicrafts are specifically broken into short lessons. The videos fit perfectly into a once-a-week viewing rotation during Morning Time. Then children can practice the skills they are learning during the other days (keeping hands busy while Mom reads aloud) and during their free time.

Language Arts

Poetry

Poetry can be intimidating to those of us raised on scavenger hunts for meaning and symbolism imposed on us by well-meaning deconstructionists. So first: don't do that to your kids. Simply read and enjoy the poems together. Point out a line or a word you like and tell why you like it—is it the sounds of the words or the comparison the poet makes? Ask the kids what they like. Really, that is all there is to good poetry study.

- ***Enjoy the Poems*** by ***Simply Charlotte Mason***—This resource provides a brief biographical sketch for a single poet plus twenty-six poems. This allows you to really get to know a poet over the course of a year. The book also includes hints for reading poems aloud and notes about language.

- ***Poetry for Young People*** Series—This series of books also provides about twenty-five poems of a specific poet selected for children. It includes biographical information and suggestions for reading specific lines.

- *Ambleside Online* **Poetry Page**—The ladies at Ambleside Online have a wonderful poetry resource with helpful articles on Charlotte Mason's philosophy about poetry, suggested poets for each year, and links to helpful resources including their own Kindle compilations of poetry.

Shakespeare

The Bard is a wonderful addition to Morning Time studies. His works so permeate our language and culture that he is vital to study every year. Contrary to popular belief, given the right attitude and approach, children love Shakespeare. Here are a few of my favorite resources to make it happen.

- *How to Teach Your Children Shakespeare*—Ken Ludwig's recitation-based technique for enjoying Shakespeare with your children is a great place to start even if you don't use all of his selections for study.

- *Shakespeare in Three Steps* by *Simply Charlotte Mason*—This guide walks you through three steps to study a Shakespeare play. First you read the story via an adaptation, second you read along while listening to *Arkangel Shakespeare* recordings, and finally you watch a video version of the play (they offer recommendations for the best adaptations for various age groups). The lessons are broken into fifteen-minute segments. Enjoy and learn Shakespeare in just 15 minutes a week!

- *Shakespeare Can Be Fun!*—These books by Lois Burdett feature adaptations told in rhyming couplets using some of the original lines from the plays. Each book is illustrated by the school children in Ms. Burdett's classes. A wonderful way to learn the stories of Shakespeare.

- **Mystie's Shakespeare Resources**—A treasure trove of even more Shakespeare resources and ideas from Mystie Winckler at *SimplyConvivial.com*.

- *Usborne* **Shakespeare Collection**—From the *Illustrated Tales from Shakespeare* to the *Shakespeare Sticker Dolly Dressing Book*, these are all favorites in our home.

- *Great Scenes from Shakespeare's Plays Coloring Book* **by** *Dover*—Perfect for coloring while listening to the stories.

Grammar

Though you will at some point in your child's education likely want to include at least a year or more of formalized grammar study, including it in Morning Time is a way to review grammar or add a light grammar introduction in the earlier grades. Grammar can be done orally, using a whiteboard to write sentences, with everyone taking turns calling out answers or writing them on the board.

- *First Language Lessons*—If you are working with a group of younger children, these oral lessons from Peace Hill Press are a great start to grammar studies. Includes memorization, picture study, and grammar, and can be done in minutes a day. Good for K-3.

- *Michael Clay Thompson Language Arts*—This delightful program is perfect for grammar during Morning Time. The program consists of a grammar story book plus an exercise book with over 100 practice sentences for four-level sentence analysis. Begin by reading through the text in small chunks. Once through the text, start practicing the four-level analysis with the practice sentences on the whiteboard once or twice a week. Model until your students become confident. Good for grades 3-8.

- *Our Mother Tongue* by **Nancy Wilson**—This brief guide to grammar basics, taught by diagramming, could easily be done orally or on a whiteboard during Morning Time.

- *Grammar Land* by **M. L. Nesbit**—This story with the parts of speech as characters is both clever and fun. There are short practice exercises at the end of each chapter for reinforcement of the concepts.

Math and Science

Math

I bet you never thought you would see this here, right? Morning Time is the perfect time to focus on the beauty and wonder in mathematics that so often gets downplayed in our mathematics curriculum. Here are a few of our favorite resources:

- *Bedtime Math*—This is a website, an app, and a series of books; so choose your favorite format. There is a mathematical story and then problems related to the story on various ability levels. An interesting tale to go with your math each day—my kids love it.

- *Time-Life I Love Math* **Books**—Sadly, these gems are out-of-print, but do look for them in your library, at thrift stores, and online, where they can often be found for a reasonable price. We open one up and the kids gather round while we read a few pages and orally do the activities together. Good for about grade three and under.

- *Penrose the Mathematical Cat*—Fun book featuring a cat and his mathematical adventures. Written at a level engaging to a child, it breaks down complex mathematical concepts, making them easier to understand (though not always completely easy for this non-math-minded mama). Includes problems at the end of each chapter to work (or not).

- *Livingmath.net* **Book List**—Fabulous resource for more mathematical readers to include during Morning Time.

- *Mathematicians Are People, Too*—Make math more human with these brief biographical stories of mathematicians from history.

- *Life of Fred*—These quirky math stories are a big hit with kids because of their humor and because of the lovable main character, Fred, a child mathematician. The books introduce interesting, higher-level math concepts in creative, approachable ways.

Science

A brief Morning Time reading session is the perfect time to read a living science book in addition to, or instead of, your normal text.

- *Macbeth's Opinion*—This website (http:// charlottemason.tripod.com/) run by homeschooling mom Macbeth Dermont is a treasure of living books suggestions for elementary and secondary science.

- *Exploring Science* **Series by John Hudson Tiner**— Written in an engaging, narrative style, the books in this series look at everything from physics to the history of mathematics. Tiner includes the history of the discoveries along with the conceptual explanations written in a clear style. These are good for middle school students, but both younger and older children will also enjoy them.

Nature Study

Yes! Nature study can be done without going on a long trek. In fact, the backyard is a wonderful place for kids to learn about nature. If even a short trip would derail your Morning Time, you can also read a nature book, make observations from your windows, or draw and study objects collected at other times.

- *Learning About Birds with Thornton Burgess*—This guide from *Simply Charlotte Mason* gives a reading schedule and nature study ideas for a year-long bird study. It encourages you to learn the birds around you by using a field guide for identification.

- *Handbook of Nature Study* **Blog**—Barb's wonderful blog has tons of ideas that can be adapted for simple Morning Time nature study without traveling far from your table.

- *Shining Dawn* **Books**—Though not designed as an "indoor" nature study, these nature guides from Cindy West are rich with information—poems, reading suggestions, notebooking pages, and nonfiction information—that can be utilized during Morning Time, with a separate observational nature trip at a different time of week.

- *One Small Square* **Series**—These lavishly-illustrated volumes are a wonderful way to study outdoor habitats while indoors, especially when you don't have access to that habitat near you.

- *Exploring Nature With Children: A Complete, Year-Long Curriculum*—This year-long nature curriculum organized by month includes observation ideas, poetry, art, and correlations to the *Handbook of Nature Study*.

History

History and historical fiction make good Morning Time read-alouds, providing fodder for interesting discussion.

- *Story of the World* **Volumes 1-4**—I love to get the audio versions of these, read by Jim Weiss. This gives my voice a brief break during Morning Time, and he just does it so much better. The activity guides come with narration question helps, map work, and supplemental historical fiction reading.

- *Stories of the Americas* **and** *Stories of the Nations*— These living book historical spines from *Simply Charlotte Mason* offer an alternative to *Story of the World*.

- *Simply Charlotte Mason Curriculum Guide*— This free online curriculum guide has living book suggestions for all ages and historical time periods.

- *Ambleside Online*—This online Charlotte Mason resource has living book history selections for all ages and historical time periods.

Faith

For many, the "ritual R" in Morning Time will be fulfilled with prayer and readings from their faith tradition. The relational aspect of Morning Time is the perfect atmosphere for those important questions and conversations that come with this subject. I have included three lists of resources for you here: first Catholic-specific resources, then Protestant and non-denominational resources provided by my friends.

Catholic Resources

- *Children's Daily Prayer*—This prayer book published by *Liturgy Training Publications* is made for schools but is easily adapted to the homeschool. It has a Gospel reading, responsorial Psalm, and reflection for every weekday, as well as prayers for different feast days and seasons in the Liturgical Year.

- *A Life of Our Lord for Children, St. Patrick's Summer,* **and other books by Marigold Hunt**— These wonderful books are interesting retellings of the life of Christ, the early Church, and our beliefs in the catechism.

- *The King of the Golden City*—An allegory for children, this engaging tale helps children understand

Holy Communion and shows how Jesus desires to have a personal relationship with them.

- ***Little Acts of Grace***—Written for younger children, this conversational little book talks about the meaning and reverence behind many of our Catholic practices.

- ***The Great Adventure Kids***—Catholic Bible study for kids based on the *Great Adventure Bible Timeline*.

- ***Read Aloud Book of Bible Stories***—This Bible story book has a fantastic narrative with beautiful and poetic language. Very easy to read aloud.

- ***Once Upon a Time Saints*** and ***More Once Upon a Time Saints***—Saint stories told in fairy tale style. Rich language and good storytelling make these an enjoyable saint study for children of any age.

- ***My Path to Heaven: A Young Person's Guide to the Faith***—This retreat-in-a-book is based on the practice of the traditional St. Ignatius retreat yet is adapted for children. It takes a practical look at the tenets of the Faith and relates them to the lives of your kids. Upper elementary and above.

Protestant Resources

- ***Songs for Saplings***—Based on *The Catechism For Young People*, these fun tunes help children memorize the catechism. The songs are catchy and provide a verse for Scripture reference.

- *The Child's Story Bible* by **Catherine Vos**—Bible stories retold for young ones.

- *Teaching Hearts, Training Minds* by **Starr Meade**— Walks you through the Westminster Shorter Catechism with short explanations of the concepts.

- *Mighty Acts of God & Wondrous Works of God* by **Starr Meade**—Bible story books that are written to demonstrate God's character.

- **Mystie's selection of Hymns, Scripture, & Catechism** to memorize at *SimplyConvivial.com*.

- *Leading Little Ones to God*—This gentle introduction to the basics of Christian teaching will help you talk to your preschoolers and young elementary students about God and salvation.

- *The Christian Almanac*—This is a fun Morning Time read-aloud in a "this day in history" format.

Non-Denominational Resources

- *Book of Virtues*—This collection by William Bennett has stories, poems, myths, and fairy tales that illustrate specific virtues.

- *Big Thoughts for Little People*—An alphabetical list of virtues and Christian practice. Each two-page spread includes a short truth like "God loves everyone" or "Do not lie," an illustration, and a series of questions about the illustration that cause children to think about the truth presented. There is also a Bible verse related to the truth as well. Perfect for the preschool/kindergarten set.

- *A Child's Book of Character Building,* Books 1 and 2—Another virtue presentation that includes stories of how the virtue unfolds at home, at play, and at school.

Whew! Keep in mind that while these are resources I have used myself or that have been recommended by my close friends, not every resource will be right for every family. It is ultimately up to you as Mom to discern which resources are a good fit for you and yours. These are also only a small selection of items available for your Morning Time. To see links to these items and more as I add them, you can visit pambarnhill.com/morningtimeresources.

Morning Time Snapshot #5: Mystie Winckler

How many kids do you have and what are their ages?

My husband and I have five kids: a boy who is 12, a boy who is 10, a girl who is 7, a boy who is 5, and a girl who is 2. Two- and three-year-olds definitely present a challenge to homeschooling in general and Morning Time in particular, but we muddle on through anyway.

How long have you been doing Morning Time?

We've been doing Morning Time since the beginning of our homeschool journey seven years ago, when my oldest was 5. We just began our eighth year of Morning Time! I read Cindy Rollin's blog faithfully since the time I found it when my oldest was three or four, and her posts about Morning Time resonated with me. So even when the weeks and even months have been difficult, I've stuck to it on faith that Cindy was right and I would regret giving up.

Now, I don't take it on faith. It has most certainly been the best part, the most fruitful part, of our homeschool; when my husband tells others about our homeschool, it is our Morning Time that he points to. We both know it is where the value is highest in our days.

What do you call your Morning Time?

When we began, I called it Circle Time. It's been Circle Time for seven years, even though I always despised the name because it sounded so preschool-y. I was brave enough this year to give our Morning Time a grown-up, classical name. We're calling it Convocation this year, and I love it; because in Latin it is "con" (together) and "vocare" (to speak), and in English it refers to calling people together for an assembly.

Typically how long does your Morning Time take on an average day?

Our Morning Time is usually between 40-50 minutes long, depending on how squirrelly the toddler is and how slow the new reader is and how well everyone is tracking. On our schedule I block an hour off for it, though, because we're all less stressed or hurried when we have margin built into the plan.

What is your favorite Morning Time subject or activity?

My favorite, can't-be-missed part of Morning Time is singing hymns together. Even though we can't keep a tune, and we sound horrible, there is something about singing together that melts bad moods and resistance and knits us together like nothing else. It is really hard to hold on to a bad attitude and sing at the same time. And, it's also hard to hold out and refuse to sing on a five- or six-verse hymn—even if some didn't want to begin, they're with us by the end.

After I noticed how strongly singing affected our moods and our unity, I changed our routine to always begin and end with a hymn. Then, if (when) people come to the table grumpy (and sometimes that person is me), they have a chance and a help to get on board; and then at the end we leave the table with that unity as the last taste left in our mouths. It is a much better mindset with which to begin a math lesson!

What is your kids' favorite Morning Time subject or activity?

My kids' favorite Morning Time activity is our new addition this year: art on an index card. As we begin, I pass an index card to everyone; and they have their crayons or pencils, and they can draw or color or scribble or write whatever they want. They do that while we listen to some memory chants and songs on the iPod together, then we transition with a "call" (Bible reading) and a hymn to our binder time. During the binder/memory-work time, if they can participate and draw at the same time,, they're free to do so. It gives them something to keep their hands occupied while their minds are active and engaged.

What is your biggest struggle with Morning Time?

Corralling and managing six people (I can be just as hard to pull to the table as the two-year-old), and bringing us all to the same place at the same time on the same page is our biggest struggle.

Starting is the hardest part of so many things in our lives, and Morning Time is no exception. I'm often tempted to skip it "just this once" or postpone it another half hour (which becomes the same thing as canceling it) or wait until I have my coffee and then not start the coffee. It seems like it will be such an exertion, such a hassle. Once we're together and have begun, it's such a blessing, and I'm so grateful for it; but having to stop the morning craziness and bring everyone together sometimes feels like too much.

How have you seen Morning Time bear fruit in your home?

I love hearing toddlers sing "Holy, Holy, Holy" in their cribs at nap time (all of ours have done so). I love hearing scraps of Shakespeare or poems or Scripture pop up in kids' play. I love that my children think poetry and prayer and catechism are normal. Most of all, however, I see the fruit of Morning Time in our shared family culture.

We have spoken the same words—mostly inspired, God-breathed words and large chunks of them—together in unison day in and day out. You can't do that without it changing you. God promises His Word never returns void, and that includes when it's recited or read in Morning Time.

What are your favorite Morning Time resources?

My first favorite is the binders which house our memory work—individual copies for each student. We also are thankful for an accompaniment CD by Susan Beisner, which makes our singing not sound as dreadful as it otherwise would. I also love having the Bible on audio (Hear the Word ESV) so I'm not talking for an hour straight.

What are some of the ritual practices you include in Morning Time?

New this year, to help my "starting is the hardest part" struggle, is how I gather everyone to the table. I was reading an early draft of Pam's *Your Morning Basket*, saw this idea, and immediately implemented it. We've been using it for over six weeks now; and it has made getting Morning Time started so much less effort, which means it's happened with so much more consistency!

Rather than trying to call everyone, interrupting that one's math drill and another one's typing practice and another one's LEGO play, trying to get everyone gathered up without each person feeling imposed upon, I simply start a fun song, Andrew Peterson's "Little Boy Heart Alive," a family favorite. It is four and a half minutes long, and when everyone hears it, they're supposed to wrap up what they're doing, grab their binder and whatever else they want to bring to the table, and be sitting at the table (with their index card to draw on) before the song is over.

So instead of yelling to be heard throughout the house or cajoling students who feel resentful of having their business interrupted, all I have to do is hit "play"—and even then I still have a minute to get my ice water and my coffee and my binder and sit down at the table—all the while maintaining my cool and not feeling frantic or like I am already worn out.

The toddler still sometimes needs cajoling, but even she now knows that song means she gets her special crayons and an index card or the container of pattern blocks or something else special to do, so she'll come running to her chair with everyone else—usually.

eleven

Morning Time Questions

I am going to start this chapter by once again emphasizing the flexibility of Morning Time. It is an important practice but also a forgiving one. Like any homeschooling practice, it should be your servant and not your master. Over time you will figure out how Morning Time works best in your family. However, if you are looking to troubleshoot common Morning Time issues, then this chapter is for you.

How long should it take?

Unfortunately there is no simple answer to that question. To begin, we must first consider the intention of the asker. For many moms, there is a practical side to the question. Time is a finite commodity on any given day, and as worthy as a practice may be, there are practical considerations to take into account before partitioning off a chunk of the schedule for anything. On the other hand, many of us ask this question in an effort to refrain from asking the real question in our hearts. I know this because it is one I sometimes struggle with myself. The question we want to ask is "How long am I supposed to take out of my day for this extra stuff before we can get to our 'real' schoolwork? Sure, all the picture study, Shakespeare, and memory work are nice; but what we really need to be doing is the next grammar lesson or another math worksheet."

There is a conflict between our modern utilitarian view of education, which has been ingrained in most of us since we first stepped on the yellow bus to ride to kindergarten, and the liberal arts tradition that we are trying to recover in practices such as Morning Time. Modern education is about creating workers to fill their role in industry and trade. Modern curriculum teaches reading comprehension skills with snippets of informational texts, tries to measure knowledge with multiple choice tests, and assigns busywork to attempt to illustrate accomplishment. A liberal arts education, on the other hand, builds virtue through habit, wisdom through communion with great thinkers in literature, and metaphorical thinking through poetry.

Morning Time looks so different than education as we know it that we struggle with recognizing it as true education at all. It could be that the tension is resolved only after long years of seeing Morning Time bear fruit in our families. It could be that the tension is never fully resolved, and this is something we always struggle with as homeschoolers. Change, especially change in attitude, is very difficult. I would ask you to consider, though, the story of Martha and Mary in the Gospel of Luke. While Martha toils in the kitchen doing the necessary tasks, she becomes anxious and upset that her sister Mary chooses to sit at the feet of their Guest and listen to Him instead. In her frustration she questions Jesus. Isn't He upset that Mary has left her to do all the preparations alone? Christ responds:

"The Lord said to her in reply, 'Martha, Martha, you are anxious and worried about many things. There is need of only one thing. Mary has chosen the better part, and it will not be taken from her'" (Luke 10:41-42).[46]

Yes, math, handwriting, and spelling are all necessary subjects. Like Martha's kitchen preparations, they must be done regularly. But are they more important than forming souls? The work of Morning Time is to behold Christ through the wonders of His world—story, art, music, nature. When viewed in this way, these subjects are not merely "add-ons" to the more important things of our day but are instead the heart of the education we want to give our children.

That said, there are some practical implications that will affect the length of our Morning Time and even how long each child spends doing it. An argument can be made that preschool should be all Morning Time with a lot of play thrown in for good measure. Throw in a craft or coloring page to develop fine motor skills, and you have a complete curriculum for the pre-kindergarten set. In this season of life, multiple Morning Time sessions full of finger plays, picture books, poetry, nature observation, and song and movement are probably better than one long session.

On the other end of the spectrum, high school students may need more time in their day to spend on those meatier works of literature not appropriate for the entire family or on more involved studies of science and mathematics. After years of Morning Time learning, there may be a point when they are released earlier to work on individual school work, while Mom continues Morning Time with the younger students. Many moms of older students talk about using this method in their Morning Time. When making a schedule, consider arranging subjects so that older students can drop off at various points of the Morning Time, if that is needed.

During a season where you have multiple young children needing a large amount of at-elbow time with Mom in order to complete skill subjects—typically children between first and fourth grade—then Morning Time may need to be a shorter affair. When more children are able to work independently during the rest of their day, then Morning Time can be lengthened again.

Nothing adds flavor to Morning Time like a rambunctious toddler. It is so very important to give yourself grace with a toddler in the mix, while nursing a new baby, or with that joyfully chaotic combination of both. During those seasons of life, do not lose heart or feel defeated if your Morning Time is a quick prayer, Scripture reading, and hymn, plus an additional read-aloud session during nap time (or better yet, an audiobook while Mom closes her eyes for a moment, too).

In addition to seasonal considerations, consider the idea of quality and not quantity when planning a Morning Time. We should focus on the best things and not try to fill our schedule with a large amount of good things. And small amounts of these best things really do go a long way. Remember the grains of sand analogy? After a while, all those tiny grains add up to an entire mountain.

Ask yourself which subjects are the most appropriate use of your time and then create your schedule around those. Our homeschool co-op teaches history through memorizing a timeline, reading and narrating picture books about historical events, and through hands-on history projects.

I supplement this at home by reading from a history spine during our Morning Time studies. I have been tempted in the past to add additional history readings to our Morning Time, but that really is unnecessary for my elementary-aged children. My oldest daughter can supplement our history by reading historical fiction on her own.

Even after careful culling of Morning Time subjects, we can also use creative scheduling techniques like block or loop scheduling to achieve a restful Morning Time. Every subject does not have to be done during every Morning Time; subjects can be alternated between various days of the week or even various terms. Review the planning chapter for exactly how to do that.

How do you get them to be still?

Two out of my three children wake up ready and raring to go each morning. They can go from dead asleep to full-on rambunctious in under 60 seconds. "Ugh" is all I can say about that. Fortunately they don't do it every morning, but they do have that capability. Whether it is a toddler who is wreaking havoc on a house for a season or simply your intuition that there is no way all of your children are going to sit still and quiet for an hour or more while listening to and reciting poetry, Rambunctious Child Syndrome is a very real obstacle to Morning Time. (Ok, I made that up, but I bet you can totally relate.) So I am going to say it right here and now in bold letters—**your children do not need to sit still and quiet for the entire Morning Time**. You can still have an effective Morning Time that includes noise, movement, and even a toddler or two.

I wish I had a magic bullet answer to the toddler issue, but sadly I do not. I have endured a number of years of bouncing toddler/preschooler during Morning Time without ever finding a perfect solution to the mayhem. The most important thing is just to push through and keep on, even if there are days when Morning Time is cut short (or purposefully planned that way) for this particular season.

In Matthew 19:13-15 some children came to see Jesus. Now we don't know much about these children—were they dressed in their best to meet the Messiah? Had they been admonished to be on their very best behavior? Maybe so, but I dress my children well and admonish them each Sunday when we go to meet Jesus in Mass, and that somehow doesn't stop them from getting wrinkled or occasionally being louder than I prefer. I imagine these children were very much like our own despite their parents' efforts—a little sticky, a little loud, a little inappropriate.

The disciples tried to shoo them away but were immediately rebuked by Jesus. He told them, "Let the children come to me, and do not prevent them; for the kingdom of heaven belongs to such as these." Jesus loved those children, and He loves ours—messy loudness and all. The key here, though, is that we have to take our children to Jesus in order for them to receive His blessing. If we never take them, they don't benefit. So persevere—get up every morning and just begin. There are graces to help pull you through. Will it be easy? No. In fact, some versions of the Bible use the words, "Suffer the children..." There are many days when suffering is what you will do, but the reward will be worth the effort.[47]

There are a few tips you can use to help make the toddler years better. One reason Mystie Winckler has a copy of her

Morning Time memory work for each student is so Morning Time can go on without her if she has to get up and leave the room with a baby or toddler. Her older children can continue to read and lead, even when she needs to change a diaper or handle a discipline issue.[48]

Always remember to plan your Morning Time for the season you are in. Start the day with a bit of ritual and a tiny bit of reading and then save other subjects for nap time, or just have a short Morning Time for a couple of years. Another possible solution that might work is to have a basket or bin of special toys and activities that only come out during Morning Time. These might hold interest long enough.

Celeste Cruz shared that she does her Morning Time during breakfast. "The reason I want to do it during breakfast is because I don't like to have my little ones have to sit down for too long. So I figured, OK, they're already sitting and eating; and that seems like a good time to throw something in there. So we always have done our Morning Basket during breakfast. And then as long as they'll kind of linger at the table, then we'll continue on; but otherwise I call it quits once everyone starts to get rowdy."[49]

If you have one who is still nursing, save Morning Time for morning snack time. Actually, this works great for older little ones as well. Snap your child in his seat and cut food into tiny pieces to be eaten one by one while Morning Time happens around him. I am going to be honest—the snack trick works for all ages at Morning Time. We love to have popcorn or hot chocolate if Morning Time is still happening about mid-morning. We just wait until recitation is over to provide the snack.

None of my children sit quietly with hands folded through

the entire Morning Time. I do require that they sit silently without distraction or activity during the prayer portion of our morning, but after that they are free to draw or play quietly at or near the table while we work. I only require that they not be doing something that distracts them—so no math, reading, or handwriting—and that they are quiet. Here are a few of their favorite activities:

- **Puzzles**—Wooden puzzles or larger floor puzzles both work well.

- **Pattern blocks**—We have the wooden blocks plus a set of mats they can use to try to complete the patterns. Many times they make creative freestyle patterns and pictures on their own.

- **Watercolors**—Not too messy, and it is easy to get the supplies out for painting.

- *Pearler Beads*—My youngest really likes to make things out of these meltable beads. He has patterns he uses, or comes up with his own.

- *Rainbow Loom*—Another son likes to loom as he recites his memory work or listens to me read aloud. He makes bracelets and charms using the colorful bands.

- **Drawing and coloring**—The kids request coloring pages online, or sometimes I provide history- or science-based ones to go with the reading. We also have a large stack of scratch paper for original creations in pencil, crayon, and colored pencil.

- *Legos* or *Magformers*—Building toys are always a hit at Morning Time.

- *Play Dough*—We usually keep a stash of homemade dough tucked under the table in a box with seasonal cookie cutters and some dough tools. You can use store-bought, but we use this easy recipe to make our own and color and scent it depending on the season. Orange pumpkin for fall. Red or green peppermint for Christmas. Yellow for summer. It really is quite easy to make.

Morning Time Play Dough

- 1 c. flour

- 1/2 cup salt

- 1 T. cooking oil

- 1 T. cream of tartar

- 1 c. water

- Food coloring of your choice (liquid or paste will work)

- Add-ins of your choice (i.e. spices, extracts, glitter, etc.)

1. Add all the dry ingredients plus the oil to a 4-quart sauce pan.

2. If using liquid food coloring, mix it in with the water and then add that combination to the pot as well.

3. If you are using spices or extracts, this is the time to add them. I start with about a tablespoon of spice or a couple of teaspoons of extract.

4. Mix together and turn the heat on about medium high at this point.

5. Heat the mixture, stirring often, until it starts to thicken and then forms a ball.

6. When done, the dough will be mostly dry but still have a few wetter spots. This is ok. You don't want it too dry.

7. Remove from heat and turn the ball of dough out onto wax paper or parchment. Yes, this sticks to your pan very badly. Scrape out what you can and then immediately set the pan to soak. When I do that, I don't have a bad time getting the pan clean.

8. Knead the dough for about 5 minutes. The more you knead, the smoother the dough will be. Caution: It will be very hot at first, so be careful not to burn your hands. This part is definitely for a grown-up. If you

are using paste-type food coloring, you can knead it in at this step.

9. Store your play dough in an airtight container or storage bag. If you keep the air out, it will last a number of months.

I have made this without cream of tartar and without oil before. Don't let not having one of them stop you from whipping up a batch. It works without either, but it is smoothest and will last the longest when you add them in. And I never make just one batch—always at least two. You can double the recipe with no problem.

Children can and do give their attention to a reading or recitation even while their hands are busy with other things. I have seen evidence that they might even pay better attention when allowed to move and do things as they listen. Don't be afraid to give it a try. With a few ground rules in place—mouth moving during recitation, no noise, listening-ears on—you may find that they are learning at a pace you would not have expected amidst the activity.

Does Morning Time have to be done in the morning? Or what if (some of) our family gets up late?

No. Morning Time doesn't have to be done in the morning or first thing in the morning. Early risers can work independently in the morning until everyone is awake. If certain members of your family sleep late, then begin once everyone is up.

A couple of things to remember: First, I do believe that Morning Time sets the learning disposition for the day. We have done Morning Time first and not first, and it is much easier by far for us to do it first. So for now I start it at 8:30 and require everyone to be present and ready to go. I know this time works for our family, and that is why I chose it. The boys and I could start Morning Time at 7:30, but I don't want to (too much of a slow mover in the morning); and my daughter is not up and ready by then. So look at your family routine and find the time that works.

Second, if you decide that the start time will be later and you want to do other things before Morning Time begins, you are going to have to practice discipline in making sure it gets done. If you can call everyone back and do it at the end, that is great. (I can't. Once the boys are done and gone, they are lost to me for the day.) Or you may have a stopping point in the middle of the morning once everyone is awake and ready and can do it then. It might help at that point to peg it to a morning snack (or breakfast for later risers).

How do you do Morning Time with a large age range? Or should I do multiple morning times with different ages?

Try a Morning Time with a graduated drop-off (yes, I made that term up). Start with the things you want to do with everyone and then decide at what points every age group can leave Morning Time. It could be that the four-year-old only has to sit for the ritual part and then can retire to the playroom with his Legos. Maybe after a few subjects together, you release teens to do independent work while you continue with the elementary-aged students. Or vice versa.

Another thing you can do is have a brief Morning Time with everyone together and then separate times for different ages. Mystie from *Simply Convivial* does this. She does Morning Time for about 30 minutes including ritual and recitation with a brief reading. All of her children do this together. After a short break she does "Couch Time," which is an extension of Morning Time for her youngest students—mostly picture books and phonics. Then twice a week she does elementary lessons in the afternoon with her school-age kids. This is where she places things like history and science readings and Shakespeare. Truly, you can create a model that works for your own family.

I think an important thing to remember is that younger kids can learn to sit and play quietly nearby while you read Shakespeare and other materials that might be "over their heads." They will soak it all in and surprise you with what they understand and remember. Kids often understand and internalize much more than we give them credit for. So begin with the expectation that they will be present but not absolutely quiet while they play, and let them be part of the learning community. They will glean what they can, and you might be surprised at how much that is.

How do I do Morning Time with an only child?

It's the same. Remember that Mom is a Morning Time participant just like any child, so your community consists of two. Read together, pray together, recite together. Take special care not to turn it into a quiz, and make sure that as Mom you are fully present and participating. Depending on her age, give the child a chance to lead a few parts of Morning Time each day.

Should I do Morning Time with my teens?

If you have gotten this far in the book (tell me you did not skip right to this section), then you know the answer to this one already. When I talk about Morning Time, I am not talking about days-of-the-week songs and carpet squares. Teens need prayer, community, and relationship just as much as anyone—perhaps even more. So yes! Do Morning Time with your teens. I will stress again Mom's role as a co-participant in Morning Time.

The teen years are fun ones for discussion as teens really begin to see things at a deeper level and wrestle intensely with those big ideas. Also, Morning Time with teens is a perfect time to give over ownership of parts of the process. Have a teen lead the prayer or read Scripture. Let them choose poems to memorize or do Shakespeare as a reader's theater with everyone taking lines. This makes Morning Time the ultimate community practice. Yes, there will come a time when their need for sleep and the requirements of their assignments may shorten your Morning Time, but to do away with it altogether would be to lose something of great value.

Where should we do Morning Time?

For a long time I had this idyllic picture in my head of all of us gathered in front of a fire on cold mornings, snuggling under a blanket, sipping hot drinks, and enjoying Morning Time together. It has remained an idyllic picture in my head. For some reason, the relaxed atmosphere of the living room wreaks havoc on any semblance of order during our Morning Time. So we do it at the table. The kids do sometimes sit on the floor to do a puzzle or dance about the room while singing, but we need the structure of the table to help keep us serious about the moment. Another option would be to peg Morning Time to breakfast. If your family eats together, it might be natural to transition right into Morning Time at the breakfast table.

Your family could very well be different, so by all means, do it in the living room, or the back porch, or on the trampoline. (We have done this a couple of times. It works as a special treat.) We can also do a fairly decent Morning Time in the car if we have to. As long as I have my playlists and audiobooks, the captive audience almost makes it easier. Do what works for you—there is no wrong answer.

How do I round up the kids for Morning Time?

Yelling like a fishmonger is no way to begin the contemplation of truth, goodness, and beauty. Having a signal that indicates the start of Morning Time is a good alternative. Cindy says she used to go around to her kids and tell them, "Five minutes until Morning Time." You could also use a bell to indicate Morning Time is about to begin. I like to play a praise song that the kids really enjoy. It always gets us happy and in the mood to begin.

What if I'm still overwhelmed, feel inadequate, or don't know where to start?

Then email me. Send an email to pam@pambarnhill.com with your questions or concerns, and give me a few days to get back to you. And pray (actually do that first) and ask the Holy Spirit to give you wisdom and guidance. Morning Time is not meant to be a new avenue of stress for your life, but instead a practice that blesses your family. Start small. Practice often. And don't forget to pray.

Morning Time Snapshot #6: Dawn Garrett

How many kids do you have and what are their ages?

I have three children, close in age. Margaret is 12, Nate is 11, and Rebekah is 9. I love having them close in age, because we can work on the same assignments and differentiate slightly.

How long have you been doing Morning Time?

We've always done some form of Morning Time. We started with Calendar Time when everyone was toddlers or younger, graduated to a "Breakfast Board" with preschoolers, and fell into our proper "Morning Time" routine in 2010. I was influenced by Cindy Rollins' blog, Kendra Fletcher's ebook *Circle Time: Plan The Best time of Your Day*, and my friend Heather's Circle Time routine.

We started pretty simply with Bible, Hymns, and poetry. Over the years, it has expanded and contracted from time to time, but we've always had those three components.

What do you call your Morning Time?

We call Morning Time "Whatchamacallit." At first, that started as a bit of a joke, because I work with so many people who use so many different names—Circle

Time, Morning Time, Morning Basket, Power Hour, Symposium, Whatchamacallit.

As I thought about it, though, it's actually a pretty good name. It's a catch-all name for a catch-all time of day. Over the course of a week, we do a little bit of almost everything during Whatchamacallit. I love how ours really includes almost everything we want to study in quick, bite-sized chunks.

Typically how long does your Morning Time take on an average day?

Our Whatchamacallit is designed to take an hour and a half. I set timers for the start and end of Whatchamacallit, and we often need them. It's the first thing we do in our school day and holds the most important elements of our day. Some parts of Whatchamacallit, like memory work, we work quickly; while others, like our read aloud, are more leisurely.

We have three thirty-minute blocks in our Morning Time. The thirty minutes are approximate, and we often skew them a little in either direction.

We spend our first half hour with Bible reading and memory, prayer, hymn singing, and catechism. Over the years, this hasn't changed a great deal. We begin with a greeting and either the Doxology or Gloria Patri. This helps all of us to remember what we are doing and be in a proper frame of mind. We then read and narrate a Psalm and read from the King James for our Ambleside readings. We pray. Then we work—learning a new hymn, reciting an old and new Bible passage, studying catechism questions and answers, reading a small bit of theology, and closing with a review hymn.

During our second half hour, we focus on academics. We read about habits/character formation, science, math, or literature; practice our poetry memorization; do either grammar or writing, dependent on the week; and review our Latin memory work. We also review our current Shakespeare memory piece. Sometimes we toss dice and find the product. This is the most likely block to expand into the next. Some days I might shorten or cut one of the elements to keep us moving.

Our final half hour, I lovingly call our "Beauty Loop." Here we focus on beautiful ideas, arts, or practices. We study Shakespeare, drawing, music appreciation, art appreciation, folksongs, or work on a handicraft. We finish this block of Whatchamacallit with a fun read-aloud novel. Sometimes I read while they draw or craft, sometimes I only read a paragraph or two (Shakespeare days, in particular), but we always have a little of our current novel.

What is your favorite Morning Time subject or activity?

I love singing hymns with my children. Which is a little crazy because I don't actually sing very well. By choosing hymns by liturgical season and/or frequency of being sung by our congregation, we have learned beloved favorites that frame our time worshipfully.

I've appreciated the inculcation of excellent theology and thinking, and while we continue to learn new hymns and review old hymns during Whatchamacallit, I love to hear my eldest playing hymns on the piano by choice, or my youngest humming a hymn tune as she plays. My son and older daughter both have been taking organ lessons, because they love the church music that is a part of their everyday lives. It has given us a common language and big grins when a familiar hymn is introduced during the worship service.

What is your kids' favorite Morning Time subject or activity?

Margaret and Nate both look forward to our read-alouds. For the last year we've been reading through Kate Seredy books, so I can't say that I blame them. I try to choose books that are beautifully written, fun, and engaging—but not literature assigned by our curriculum. These books are actually what *Ambleside Online* calls "Free Reads," so they're perfect. We're currently reading *The Chestry Oak*. I want to copy almost all of it into my Commonplace book (a book for recording quotes I want to remember), it's so achingly lovely.

Rebekah loves variety and beautiful things. Her favorite part of Whatchamacallit is the Beauty Loop. She likes working on the different aspects we study but especially drawing and art appreciation.

What is your biggest struggle with Morning Time?

During Whatchamacallit, I do not require my children to sit still in their seats and hold nothing in their hands, but sometimes all of us take advantage of that. I use my phone for some of the readings—both the King James Bible and poetry books we read are on Kindle—but that means that Instagram and Facebook are at my fingertips. My children often color or draw or craft during Whatchamacallit, but that means that sometimes they walk around to get other parts and pieces. Our biggest struggle is definitely making sure everyone is doing the work at hand. I mostly allow the moving around and fiddling to go on and just watch and listen closely for participation with words and voices.

Sometimes that gets out of hand. I struggle with the divergence between my expectations and their behavior. Some days they go beyond the pale in their movements and lack of attention, and we have to regroup.

How have you seen Morning Time bear fruit in your home?

All those hymns we've sung? When they are sung in church, my kids get big smiles and winks and nudges in the pew. I hear phrases of poetry we've learned coming out in their talk at the dinner table "Theirs not to reason why, theirs but to do and die" from "The Charge of the Light Brigade" being a recent example. My youngest told me during a walk yesterday that she likes to "galumph"— from "Jabberwocky," of course. I see a love of music and the organ in my two older children, particularly, and I attribute that to highlighting hymns at an early age. But even if I didn't see fruit now, I would still see the value in being together, reading God's word, and singing His praises together. That we've added and expanded beyond that to learning a vast array of other things together is beautiful to me.

What are some of your favorite Morning Time resources?

IEW's Linguistic Development through Poetry Memorization was the first curriculum I purchased as a homeschooler and remains one of my favorites. We're having a lot of fun with the Childcraft book, *Mathemagic.* I love doing grammar during Whatchamacallit, and we use *Memoria Press' Grammar Recitation* because it has a question/answer catechismal feel that fits with our other morning time practices. On opposite weeks, *Writing and Rhetoric* has been a great way to include writing instruction during Whatchamacallit. I read sections from *The Handbook of Nature Study* by Anna Bosford Comstock, which has helped us add nature study.

Mystie's Shakespeare instruction resources are a great fit for Morning Time. Finally, I wrote an ebook about the theological underpinning to Charlotte Mason's motto, *I Am, I Can, I Ought, I Will: Charlotte Mason's Motto Explained for Upper Elementary Students.*

What are some of the ritual practices you include in Morning Time?

We open with a greeting that I learned from Kortney Garrison on the *Homeschool Snapshots Podcast.* I say "Let us remember," and they respond "that we are in the presence of the Holy God." Then we sing either the Doxology or the Gloria Patri.

Our school day itself is bracketed with this at the beginning of Whatchamacallit; then when all of their work is finished, we end with "The Lord be with you"—"And also with you." To some extent it's ritualized, because we have a defined order of practice every day, a liturgy. But that opening ritual has become so very important to all of us.

Afterword

I am sometimes astounded by the power of Morning Time. I get emails, comments, and even moms who come up to me in person who tell me about the changes that Morning Time has brought to their homeschools. It brings delight where there once was drudgery, order where there once was discord, and relationship where there once was stress. If excellence is a habit, then we reach excellence with the best habits—like Morning Time.

Appendix A:
Even More Things to Do in Your Morning Time

1. *Big Truths for Little Kids: Teaching Your Children to Live for God*—A catechism exploration book for the youngest Morning Time students. Based on *The Children's Catechism*.

2. *Little Pilgrim's Progress: From John Bunyan's Classic*—Very short chapters make this version of *Pilgrim's Progress* perfect for Morning Time. We used it as a narration exercise as well.

3. *How God Used A Thunderstorm and Other Devotional Stories*—Stories meant to tell a truth. Some are encouraging, others are instructive. The shortest story is a few paragraphs, the longest a couple of pages. Questions at the end of each story help to cement the main point. Or simply narrate the story together.

4. *The Catholic Bible for Children*—A story Bible for Catholic families to read and enjoy.

5. *Saints for Young Readers for Everyday*—Short biographies of saints geared for upper elementary students, but they work for a variety of ages.

6. Printable Rosary Cards at *thekennedyadventures.com*— Dianna Kennedy has made these fun cards to help little ones learn the mysteries of the Rosary.

7. *We Choose Virtues*—This curriculum or card set teaches virtues like patience, kindness, and diligence through fun characters and short sayings. It even features a CD of songs arranged by Pam!

8. *Laying Down the Rails* from *simplycharlottemason. com*—Habit training for what you ought to do is an important part of a child's education. This resource helps with this seemingly daunting task.

9. *The Valley of Vision: A Collection of Puritan Prayers & Devotions*—Read or memorize prayers from this little book, and you and your children will never want for rich language in your prayer life. Use as models for prayer or just discuss the spiritual truths you find.

10. *The Family Worship Book* by Terry Johnson—An all-inclusive resource to help you build a worship time into your Morning Time. Scripture memorization lists, hymns, psalms, and responsive readings help you make morning worship meaningful for your kids.

11. *The Boys and Girls Plutarch*—A version of Plutarch edited for boys and girls. Perhaps a bit less intimidating than the original.

12. *Exploring Nature With Children*—A fun and inclusive nature curriculum that allows you to do as much or as little as you have time for.

13. *Handbook of Nature Study* by Anna Comstock—A reference book for when you want to know more about a subject you are studying within any nature curricula.

14. *The Insect Folk* by Margaret Warner Morley—Fun short stories about different insects. The narrator is a teacher talking with her students as they explore. Conversational and available on *Librivox* and *Amazon Kindle* for free.

15. *Favorite Thornton Burgess Animal Stories Boxed Set*—My children adore these fun stories. They are instructive but accessible to even the youngest children and interesting enough to keep older kids listening.

16. *Parables from Nature* by Mrs. Alfred Gatty—Learning about nature through stories is always fun. This book teaches from a creation standpoint the wonders of God's world.

17. *The Story Book of Science* by Jean Henri Fabe—More science nature stories told in a conversational way.

18. *Christian Liberty Nature Reader Book 1* by Wendy Kramer—There are five of these books in total. They

are great for younger students to feature their reading ability in Morning Time as they read aloud to others.

19. *Sibley Backyard Birding* Flashcards—We love using these in Morning Time. They are fun to look at and can be passed around the table. Choose a few that you know will be in your area and branch off from there learning a few more each month.

20. *Pond and Stream* by Arthur Ransome—This is a *Simply-Charlotte-Mason*-suggested book.

21. *The Tarantula in My Purse: and 172 Other Wild Pets* by Jean Craighead George—Just a fun and funny look at nature in the life of a favorite author.

22. *God's World News For Kids*—Stay up to date with news from around the world in a kid-friendly way. There are versions for preschool and early elementary, upper elementary, and teens.

23. *Our Island Story* by H.E. Marshall—Short chapters with good stopping points make this a great Morning Time addition.

24. *50 Famous Stories Retold* by James Baldwin—A wide variety of short history stories that hold the attention of my first-grade boy amazingly well. He loves them! Some you will recognize, some may be new to you.

25. *Elementary Geography* by Charlotte Mason—These are very short lessons meant for young elementary children. They are conversational, and there are review questions to help with the discussion.

26. Continent *GeoPuzzles*—Do as a separate activity when introducing countries or allow children to put them together while you read. Either way, a great addition to your Morning Time.

27. Maps from *Notebooking Pages*—Good solid continent maps plus a whole slew of other awesome notebooking pages.

28. *Minn of the Mississippi* by Holling C. Holling—Learn the history and geography of the Mississippi. Every chapter is short and has lovely illustrations. *Paddle to the Sea* is another by Holling about the Great Lakes region. These are truly gorgeous books.

29. *Draw Europe* by Kristin J. Draeger—Practice map drawing with this series. With practice this method is easy and it works! There are books for five of the seven continents at the moment.

30. *Famous Men of Rome* by John H. Haaren—These stories are not long but pack quite a punch with possible discussions on virtue, strength, honor, civic duty, and government.

31. *Famous Men of Greece* by John H. Haaren—We haven't used this one yet but I imagine it is just as good as the above.

32. *A Year of Art Journaling*—Art for older students. Experiment with texture, color, and more with your older students as they discover or hone their artistic tendencies.

33. *What Do You See*—From *Trivium Pursuit*, this little volume is geared for your youngest students but would also be good for teaching most elementary students how to look at art.

34. *ICAN Index Card a Day*—The "Index-Card-A-Day Challenge" at *daisyyellowart.com* is a great way to stretch those creative muscles in a low-risk, small size format.

35. *Creativebug*—This online tutorial website has affordable subscription options and video classes on drawing, painting, and any number of handicrafts.

36. *Maestro Classics* CD's—A fun and entertaining way to introduce your children to music. The stories help your children begin to identify composers and pieces in an enjoyable way. Along the same line are the *Classical Kids* story CD's.

37. *Hooked on Classics*—Lively and upbeat. The perfect songs to use as your "Call to Morning Time."

38. *Listen While We Sing*—A resource for singing hymns in your morning time. Accompaniment CDs are referenced to the *Trinity Hymnal* and other popular hymnals.

39. *Simply Charlotte Mason Singing the Great Hymns*—For those who want a hymn study all laid out with a CD accompaniment.

40. *Simply Charlotte Mason Music Study with the Masters*—A lovely introduction to classical composers. Choose one or two for the year and really delve into their work.

41. *Wee Sing America*—Just for fun. Patriotic songs like "Yankee Doodle" and "You're a Grand Old Flag" are sure to get your Morning Time hopping. Check out the other volumes. This series is very well done and my kids love it.

42. *Classics for Kids* Podcast—When you want a break from reading in your Morning Time these are the perfect interlude. Quick 5-10 minute podcasts give you a break but keep your Morning Time flowing well.

43. *Math Dice*—Quick and fun to play, you can pick these dice up at *Amazon* or an educational shop. The set will come with a pamphlet of different games to play. Sneaking in a little math in Morning Time is always a good thing!

44. *Addition Facts That Stick* by Kate Snow—This little volume has games for memorizing math facts that can be done in 15-20 min. Perfect for those who need just a little extra math help. Pairing younger children with older children make this a perfect Morning Time activity. It is a good review for older kids as well.

45. *Inchimals*—Learn measurement with fun animal measuring sticks. Each animal represents a certain number of inches from 1-12. Great for adding, subtracting, and comparing.

46. *The Number Devil: A Mathematical Adventure* by Hans Magnus Enzensberger—Numbers and more numbers! Look at everything numbers can do with this resource. Good for those who love to play with numbers and those who don't.

47. Stuart Murphy *MathStart* picture books—Wildly colorful and just plain fun, add one of these as a way to reinforce and enjoy math together.

48. *The Random House Book of Poetry for Children*—This book of poetry has never disappointed us. We love the mix of classic and new poems, the seasonal poems, and those just for everyday.

49. *Favorite Poems Old and New* by Helen Ferris— Another great anthology of poems with works by Shakespeare and Tolkien.

50. *The Roar on the Other Side: A Guide for Student Poets* by Suzanne Underwood Rhodes—A resource to explore poetry with older students.

51. *A Widening Light: Poems of the Incarnation* by Lucy Shaw—Recommended by Nicholas Ireland in YMB episode #8. A good resource for older students.

52. *Linguistic Development Through Poetry Memorization*—Andrew Pudewa of the *Institute for Excellence in Writing* makes poetry memorization easy. The audio CD's are delightful. My children love to listen to them in the car.

53. *52 Weeks of Family French*—We enjoy learning French as a family. It is fun to use short small phrases together. Even my four-year-old enjoys asking to be excused from the table in a foreign language. Be sure to check out the other languages.

54. *Song School Latin*—Latin for the youngest students with fun songs and chants. The workbook can be used as a guide for review.

55. *Race to the Colosseum* Game from *pambarnhill.com*—A fun game for Latin review. Use it for Latin as well as other subjects.

56. *Learn French with Stories for Beginners*—A book with an audio CD make for an awesome Morning Time resource. There is also a Spanish version.

57. *Getting Started with Latin: Beginning Latin for Homeschoolers and Self-Taught Students of Any Age* by William E. Linney—An easy-to-use introduction to Latin vocabulary and grammar. Short lessons for your Morning Time.

58. *I Speak Latin, Living Latin for Young Learners*—A conversational Latin course that connects Latin words directly with the things, actions, or ideas they represent without using the native language.

59. *The Fallacy Detective*—This is a fun logic resource to use with middle grade to high school kids. It is best enjoyed as a family.

60. *Arkangle Shakespeare*—Fully dramatized plays on CD or for download. Listen and follow along a bit every day. There is one for every play.

61. *Mad Libs*—Sometimes you just need a break. *Mad Libs* are a quick way to break up the subjects and practice grammar at the same time.

62. *D'Aulaires' Book of Greek Myths*—Wonderfully illustrated and expertly told, there is a reason these authors are famous in homeschooling circles.

63. *Grimm's Fairy Tales*—We have an old copy of *Grimm's Fairy Tales* and have begun reading them this year. Some are good, some are weird, and some are very anticlimactic; but we have enjoyed them all.

64. *English Grammar Recitation* from *Memoria Press*—
Learn the rules of grammar in order to be successful
at a more advanced level of diagramming and
constructing sentences.

65. *Little Britches* by Ralph Moody—Highly
recommended for those who have finished *Little
House on the Prairie*. Just a good solid life story told
well.

66. *100 Cupboards* by N.D. Wilson—Probably one of my
favorite series ever. This read aloud has captured the
attention of all of my children, boys and girls, ages
four to ten. Don't let the cover scare you—so far no
nightmares.

67. *My Father's Dragon* by Ruth Stiles Gannett—Along
with the sequels, this book will be loved by your
children for years to come. Good to read for all ages.
The humor and charm never get old.

68. *The Complete Tales of Winnie-The-Pooh* by A.A.
Milne—Best read starting around 8, the humor of
Pooh is also good for many ages. It is especially good
for keeping teenagers young.

69. *On the Edge of the Dark Sea of Darkness* by Andrew
Peterson—Loved by many many families, this series is
likened to *Narnia*. I think it has a bit more humor to
it; it is also a bit sadder in some places.

70. *The Prairie Thief* by Melissa Wiley—Girls and boys will enjoy this good old-fashioned prairie story with a magical twist.

71. *Mind Trap Brain Teaser* Board Game—A classic set of brain teasers. Don't play the game in Morning Time; just read a puzzle or two to change things up a bit. Everyone can guess and work together to find the answer.

72. *Rubik's Cube*—For those who love a good puzzle and need something to keep their hands busy while listening to Morning Time readings.

73. *Castle Logix*—A fun do-it-yourself game based on castles and logic.

74. *Melissa and Doug* Floor Puzzles—With so many subjects to choose from and several different piece counts, there is a puzzle for your Morning Time. Preschoolers especially do well with these large pieces.

75. *Dover* Coloring Books—There is quite possibly one of these in every subject. I like to get one or two per kid each year. I usually choose something that relates to what we might cover in Morning Time. Colored pencils or thin markers are a must for these books.

76. *Melissa & Doug* Pattern Blocks and Boards—Keeps fingers busy but ears ready to listen.

77. *Handicrafts Made Simple* from *Simply Charlotte Mason*—If you are wondering about handicrafts, this video collection is your resource for teaching the things you never knew.

Appendix B:
100 Things for Kids to Memorize

Scripture

We start with the Holy Grail (so to speak) of memorizing—Scripture. Hiding God's Word in your heart is a necessary tool. By becoming intimately familiar with Scripture, we are able to shape our souls through the mental discipline of memorizing. If you memorize nothing else, start with these.

1. John 3:16

2. John 11:25,26

3. John 1:1-18

4. John 14:1-6

5. Ephesians 2:8-9

6. Galatians 5:22,23

7. Psalm 1

8. Psalm 100

9. Psalm 8

10.   Psalm 103

11.   Proverbs 3:5,6

12.   Romans 12

13.   Exodus 20:1-17—The Ten Commandments

14.   Matthew 5:3-12—The Beatitudes

15.   1 Corinthians 13

16.   Matthew 22:36-40

17.   Joshua 1:9

18.   Romans 10:9-11

19.   Genesis 1

20.   Ephesians 6:10-18

21.   2 Peter 1:5-9

22.   Matthew 6:1-15

23.   Matthew 22:36-40

Science Facts

Of all the memory work, I think my kids have some of the most fun with science facts. There is something about knowing those little factual tidbits that is just fun for them. Maybe it's because we often turn them into a song or a cheer. The list of scientific facts you could memorize is endless, but here are some practical ones to get you started.

1. Names and Order of Planets

2. Classification of Living Things

3. Names of the Human Systems

4. Periodic Table of Elements

5. Newton's Laws of Motion

6. Biomes

7. Laws of Thermodynamics

Poetry

Poetry is one of those things that spans the generations. Many poems will bring a smile both to a child hearing it for the first time and the adult sharing it with them. The rhythmic nature of poetry makes it an easy choice to memorize, so if you are at all intimidated by memorization, then start here.

1. "Gunga Din" by Rudyard Kipling

2. "If" by Rudyard Kipling

18. "There Was a Little Girl" by Henry Wadsworth Longfellow

19. "There Was an Old Man with a Beard" by Edward Lear

20. "The Vulture" by Hilaire Belloc

21. "The Mist and All" by Dixie Willson

Shakespeare

Ah yes, he deserves his own category. The Bard offers hundreds of choices of beautiful, quality language to add to the memory banks. Don't hesitate to give your children Shakespeare. They do not know to be intimidated and will soak it up. My seven-year-old proved that recently at an event with friends where he recited a passage from "A Midsummer Night's Dream" to an audience.

1. St. Crispin's Day Speech from *Henry V* (*Henry V*, Act IV, Scene 3, lines 18–67)

2. Balcony Scene from *Romeo and Juliet* (*Romeo and Juliet*, Act II, Scene 2 lines 1ff))

3. The Advice of Polonius (*Hamlet*, Act I, Scene 3, lines 65-86)

4. Hamlet's "To be or not to be" soliloquy (*Hamlet*, Act III, Scene 1, lines 64-76)

5. MacBeth's "Tomorrow and tomorrow and tomorrow" (*Macbeth*, Act V, Scene 5, lines 18-28)

6. "All the world's a stage, and all the men and women merely players. They have their exits and their entrances; And one man in his time plays many parts." *(As You Like It)*

7. "Life's but a walking shadow, a poor player, that struts and frets his hour upon the stage, and then is heard no more; it is a tale told by an idiot, full of sound and fury, signifying nothing." *(Macbeth)*

8. "Love looks not with the eyes, but with the mind; and therefore is winged Cupid painted blind." *(A Midsummer Night's Dream)*

9. Sonnet 18

10. Sonnet 73

Documents

By no means do we recommend that you memorize every single word, but these documents, both religious and secular, contain portions that are good to know. Choose your favorite parts and learn them.

1. Catechism—Choose the one most closely affiliated with your faith tradition.

2. Preamble to the Constitution

3. Bill of Rights

4. Declaration of Independence

Speeches

Many of these are very long. You can often find worthy excerpts online. Another great resource is *The American Heritage Book of Great American Speeches for Young People* by Suzanne McIntire.

1. "The Gettysburg Address" by Abraham Lincoln

2. "I Have a Dream" by Martin Luther King

3. Patrick Henry's "Give Me Liberty or Give me Death!"

4. The Sermon on the Mount

5. "Funeral Oration" by Pericles

6. "Remarks at the Brandenburg Gate" by Ronald Reagan

7. Resignation Speech of George Washington

8. Farewell Address by Dwight D. Eisenhower

9. Inauguration Address by John F. Kennedy

Math

No, not nearly as fun as poetry, but oh so necessary. The working memory only has so much room. In order to have room to do advanced computation, free up space in the working memory by creating instant recall of mathematical facts and formulas. Math will be so much easier on everyone.

1. Skip Counting Tables

2. Metric Conversions

3. Equivalents

4. Communicative Law

5. Associative Law

6. Distributive Law

7. Order of Operations

8. Roman Numerals

9. Quadratic Formula

10. Pi

Quotes

This category is a fun one. Our ideas will get you started, but don't forget to add more of your own favorites and have your children choose favorites of their own as they get older.

1. "It's like in the great stories, Mr. Frodo. The ones that really mattered, full of darkness and danger they were. Sometimes you didn't want to know the end, because how could the end be happy? How could the world go back to the way it was when there's so much bad that had happened? But in the end it's only a passing thing, this shadow; even darkness must pass." — Samwise Gamgee

2. "Deeds will not be less valiant because they are unpraised." — Aragorn

3. "Thou hast made us for thyself, O Lord, and our heart is restless until it finds its rest in thee." — Augustine of Hippo, *The Confessions of Saint Augustine*

4. "True humility is not thinking less of yourself; it is thinking of yourself less." — C.S. Lewis, *Mere Christianity*

5. "Fable is more historical than fact, because fact tells us about one man and fable tells us about a million men." — G.K. Chesterton

6. "Better be wise by the misfortunes of others than by your own." — Aesop

History and Geography

Probably one of the most practical and necessary of all the categories, history and geography facts provide a huge source of context for what your kids will learn in all walks of life.

1. Presidents

2. A history timeline

3. States and capitals

4. Major landforms

5. Locations of the countries of the world

English Grammar

I teach an English grammar and writing class at our co-op. I can tell you from experience that the kids who have the following lists memorized are having a much easier time diagramming sentences and discussing their writing than the kids who do not. Handy lists, these.

1. "To be" verbs

2. Prepositions

3. Coordinating conjunctions

4. Subordinating conjunctions

5. Pronouns

Endnotes

1. Pamela Barnhill, "HSP 36 Kortney Garrison: Homeschooling—Just DIY Learning," https://pambarnhill.com/hsp36/, (October, 2016).

2. Pamela Barnhill, "YMB #5 Big Family Morning Time: A Conversation with Angela Boord," https://pambarnhill.com/ymb5/, (October, 2015).

3. Barnhill, YMB #5, (October, 2015).

4. Sonya Shafer, "Facts vs. Ideas," https://simplycharlottemason.com/blog/facts-vs-ideas/, (October, 2011).

5. Charlotte Mason, *Towards a Philosophy of Education*, (London, England, 1925), 109.

6. Pamela Barnhill, "YMB #12 Teaching From Rest with Morning Time: A Conversation with Sarah Mackenzie," https://pambarnhill.com/ymb12/, (February, 2016).

7. C.S.Lewis, *The Abolition of Man*, (San Francisco, CA, 1943), 13.

8. C.S.Lewis, *The Abolition of Man*, 13.

9. Pamela Barnhill, "YMB #12: Teaching From Rest with Morning Time: A Conversation with Sarah Mackenzie," (February, 2016).

10. Pamela Barnhill, "YMB #12," (February, 2016).

11. Pamela Barnhill, "YMB #6: Jennifer Mackintosh: A Considered Book-List," https://pambarnhill.com/ymb6/, (November, 2015).

12. Pamela Barnhill, "YMB #5," (October, 2015).

13. Pamela Barnhill, "YMB #6," (November, 2015).

14. Cindy Rollins, "The Long Haul: On Morning Time," https://www.circeinstitute.org/media/audio/long-haul-morning-time, (Louiville, KY, 2012).

15. Charlotte Mason, *School Education*, (London, England, 1907), 66.

16. Stratford Caldecott, *Beauty in the Word: Rethinking the Foundations of Education,* (Tacoma, Washington, 2012), 14.

17. Aristotle, *Nicomachean Ethics, Book II, 4*, http://classics.mit.edu/Aristotle/nicomachaen.2.ii.html.

18. C.S. Lewis, *The Abolition of Man*, (San Francisco, CA), 18.

19. John14:6, NAB.

20. 2 Samuel 7:28, NAB.

21. Stratford Caldecott, *Beauty in the Word*, 142.

22. *United States Catholic Catechism for Adults*, (Washington, D.C., 2006), 320.

23. Stratford Caldecott, *Beauty for Truth's Sake*, (Grand Rapids, MI, 2009), 31.

24. Stratford Caldecott, *Beauty for Truth's Sake*, 32.

25. Mortimer J. Adler, *Six Great Ideas*, (New York, NY, 1981), 114-115.

26. Pamela Barnhill, "HSP006 Jen Dunlap: More than Enough Love," https://pambarnhill.com/6/, (January 2015).

27. James K.A. Smith, "Love Takes Practice: Liturgy, Formation, and Counter-Formation," in *Desiring the Kingdom: Worship, Worldview, and Cultural Formation*, (Grand Rapids, MI, 2009), 75-88.

28. Pamela Barnhill, "YMB #30: Tension in Morning Time: A Conversation with Jennifer Dow," https://pambarnhill.com/ymb30/, (February, 2017).

29. Pamela Barnhill, "YMB #29: Building Family Culture: A Conversation with Audrey Wilkerson," https://pambarnhill.com/ymb29/, (February, 2017).

30. Pamela Barnhill, "YMB #10: All About Narration: A Conversation with Sonya Shafer," https://pambarnhill.com/ymb10/, (January, 2016).

31. Stephen R. Turley, Ph.D., *Awakening Wonder: A Classical Guide to Truth, Goodness, and Beauty*, (Camp Hill, PA, 2014), 66.

32. Pamela Barnhill, "HSP 13 Erin Hassett: Living the Large Family Life," https://pambarnhill.com/13/, (May 2015).

33. Susan Wise Bauer, *The Well-Trained Mind*, (New York, NY), 55.

34. Pamela Barnhill, "YMB #10," (January, 2016).

35. Luke 6:31, NAB.

36. Exodus 20:12, NAB.

37. Brandy Vencel, "Memorization and the Soul," https://afterthoughtsblog.net/product/memorization-and-the-soul, (2012).

38. Andrew Pudewa, "Nurturing Competent Communicators," http://iew.com/shop/products/nurturing-competent-communicators-andrew-pudewa, (2015)

39. Robert Frost, "Stopping By Woods on a Snowy Evening," https://www.poetryfoundation.org/poems/42891/stopping-by-woods-on-a-snowy-evening, from *The Poetry of Robert Frost*, (1923).

40. Andrew Pudewa, *Linguistic Development Through Poetry Memorization*, (Oklahoma, 2016).

41. *Simply Charlotte Mason*, "Scripture Memory System," https://simplycharlottemason.com/timesavers/memorysys/, (2012).

42. Mystie Winckler, "Circle Time: Pretty, Happy, Funny, Real, Exhausting," https://www.simplyconvivial.com/2013/circle-time-pretty-happy-funny-real-exhausting, (January, 2013).

43. *Simply Charlotte Mason*, "Scripture Memory System," https://simplycharlottemason.com/timesavers/memorysys/, (2012).

44. Cindy Rollins, "What is Morning Time and Why Bother?," http://www.ordo-amoris.com/2014/08/what-is-morning-time-and-why-bother.html, (August, 2014).

45. Pamela Barnhill, "YMB #12," (February, 2016).

46. Luke 10:41-42, NAB.

47. Matthew 19:13-15, NAB.

48. Mystie Winckler, "Circle Time: Pretty, Happy, Funny, Real, Exhausting," (January, 2013).

49. Pamela Barnhill, "YMB #15: Morning Time with Littles: A Conversation with Celeste Cruz," https://pambarnhill.com/ymb15/, (March, 2016).

About Pam

Pam Barnhill is a homeschool mom and former teacher. When not teaching her three kids, she can be found writing about Morning Time and encouragement for homeschool moms at *pambarnhill.com*. She is the host of *Your Morning Basket*, a podcast devoted to helping homeschoolers contemplate truth, goodness, and beauty in Morning Time, and *The Homeschool Snapshots Podcast* where she interviews homeschooling moms, providing a peek into their homeschool days. She lives with her husband and children in beautiful Alabama.

Acknowledgments

My world is wrapped up in three beautiful children. Thank you, Olivia, John, and Thomas, for what *you* teach *me* each day.

I also could not do the things I do without my husband, Matt, who indulges most of my whims and understands my need for something of my own. I just can't thank him enough.

So many homeschool mamas have helped, aided, and encouraged me in writing this book. I couldn't have done it without Sarah Mackenzie, Jessica Lawton, Dawn Garrett, Mystie Winckler, Brandy Vencel, and Ann Karako. Mary Reiter and Tara Maple provided help with the first edition of this book and their influence carries over to this edition. In addition I would like to thank the podcast guests whose stories I include here, the Morning Time snapshot authors, and the moms in the Your Morning Basket Moms Facebook group, who were a great sounding board through the writing process.